"In *Poetry Pauses*, Vogelsinger provides exactly the encouragement, guidance, and resources that teachers of writing need. He is a master reader and master teacher—practical and accessible, nuanced and detailed. From content that students will love to assessments that will challenge them, from first principles of understanding to subtle approaches for analysis, Vogelsinger thinks like the veteran practitioner and generous colleague that all departments need. *Poetry Pauses* is a collection of resources and inspiration that I am certain will enliven and enrich my courses right away, and for years to come."

—Joel Garza
Upper School English chair, Greenhill School, Addison, TX

"Brett Vogelsinger's *Poetry Pauses* is the book we need right now to guide us in how to bring poetry into our classrooms every day not as a full-scale unit of study but by 'opening little nooks of space for poetry.' Brett's practical 'poetry pauses' give us an accessible framework and an abundance of ideas and materials for supporting students not only as poets but also as writers in all genres throughout the school year."

—Georgia Heard
Co-author, *A Field Guide to the Heart:*
Poems of Love, Comfort & Hope

"I have a few teaching books that sit right next to my desk. Tattered and dog-eared and covered in tabs, these are my go-to resources that I use again and again. *Poetry Pauses* is the newest member of this shelf. In it, Vogelsinger offers practical, vibrant lessons for using poetry to enhance everything I want to do: help students learn about language, brainstorm new ideas, sharpen claims, encounter different perspectives, hold on to feedback, engage in deep thinking, build skills, and lay the foundation for living better, richer, and more poetic lives."

—Matthew Johnson
Co-author, *Answers to Your Biggest Questions About*
Teaching Middle and High School ELA

"*Poetry Pauses* beckons us away from our classroom routines to learn in the presence of a poem. Here you will marinate in surprising language. You will laugh. You will imagine new lessons in all genres. You might grab a pen and drop a few lines. I did. Keep this on your desk; you will return often."

—Penny Kittle
Author, *Book Love and Write Beside Them*

"Brett Vogelsinger's passion for poetry bleeds through every page of *Poetry Pauses*. Poems have long often been thought of as scary or boring and using Brett's ideas in this book are sure to get your students—and YOU—to fall in love with the beauty of poetry. I can't wait to share this book with every teacher I know!"

—Todd Nesloney
Director of Culture & Strategic Leadership, TEPSA

"Writing, like teaching, is a mixture of art and science. So many professional texts make writing scientific—practical, discrete steps that can be broken down and easily taught to any student. In *Poetry Pauses*, Brett Voeglsinger brings the art and magic and mystery of writing back to our classrooms. This practical and beautiful book invites us to look at poetry in a new way. It nudges us to consider that poetry is not just a genre to be studied one month a year, but a genre that unlocks possibilities for student writers at every stage of the writing process—from planning to drafting to polishing. *Poetry Pauses* reminds us once again that poetry is a vehicle through which we can teach 'every essential feature' of writing in any genre and can be the 'foundation for a year of motivated writing' (Atwell 2015, 317-318). This book will live on the corner of my desk to be used every day in my teaching."

—Rebekah O'Dell
Co-author, *Writing with Mentors* and *Beyond Literary Analysis*

"Poetry, and taking time to pause, is a powerful ally in the endeavor to strengthen student writing. Vogelsinger's work is jam-packed with protocols, activities, resources, and just the right amount of research that will not only meet your students' writing needs, but also their need to connect to self, SEL, and society."

—Andy Schoenborn
National Writing Project Teacher Consultant and teacher at Clare Public Schools, Clare, MI

poetry pauses

poetry pauses

Teaching With Poems to Elevate Student Writing in All Genres

brett vogelsinger

Includes
100+ poems
online

CORWIN Literacy

For information:

Corwin
A SAGE Company
2455 Teller Road
Thousand Oaks, California 91320
(800) 233–9936
www.corwin.com

SAGE Publications Ltd.
1 Oliver's Yard
55 City Road
London EC1Y 1SP
United Kingdom

SAGE Publications India Pvt. Ltd.
Unit No 323–333, Third Floor,
F-Block
International Trade Tower
Nehru Place
New Delhi 110 019
India

SAGE Publications Asia-Pacific
Pte. Ltd.
18 Cross Street #10–10/11/12
China Square Central
Singapore 048423

President: Mike Soules
Vice President and Editorial
    Director: Monica Eckman
Executive Editor: Tori Mello
    Bachman
Content Development Editor:
    Sharon Wu
Editorial Assistant: Nancy Chung
Project Editor: Amy Schroller
Copy Editor: Colleen Brennan
Typesetter: Integra
Proofreader: Rae-Ann Goodwin
Indexer: Integra
Cover Designer: Gail Buschman
Marketing Manager: Margaret
    O'Connor

Copyright © 2023 by Corwin Press, Inc.

Printed in Canada

Library of Congress Cataloging-in-Publication Data

Names: Vogelsinger, Brett, author.
Title: Poetry pauses : teaching with poems to elevate student writing in all genres / Brett Vogelsinger.
Description: Thousand Oaks, California : Corwin, [2023] | Includes bibliographical references.
Identifiers: LCCN 2022050155 | ISBN 9781071889022 (paperback ; acid-free paper) | ISBN 9781071907207 (epub) | ISBN 9781071907214 (epub) | ISBN 9781071907221 (pdf)
Subjects: LCSH: English language--Rhetoric--Study and teaching--Activity programs. | Academic writing--Study and teaching--Activity programs. | Poetry--Study and teaching.
Classification: LCC PE1404 .V635 2023 | DDC 808/.042071--dc23/eng/20221129
LC record available at https://lccn.loc.gov/2022050155

This book is printed on acid-free paper.

23 24 25 26 27 10 9 8 7 6 5 4 3 2 1

CONTENTS

Visit the companion website for downloadable resources at
resources.corwin.com/poetrypauses.

ACKNOWLEDGMENTS

Thank you, thank you, thank you:

To my wife, Nichole, who showed me it was possible to bring a book into the world, and for putting up with the fevered fugues of writing and the related spaciness.

To my two sons for all the laughter and joy and wonder we share, for teaching me new things about teaching and learning, and for your poems.

To my parents for encouraging me to write and engaging me with words early in my life. To my siblings for their support and encouragement, always.

To Rebekah O'Dell for prodding me to pursue this concept for a book, and for being the reader of my earliest drafts. To Michelle Ambrosini and Molly Rickert and Zach Sibel and Louisa Irele for reading the earliest iterations of this book and offering feedback. To Chris McGullam for the walk-and-talk thinking sessions that carried me through teaching and writing in a pandemic.

To everyone at Corwin Press for their patience and trust with a newbie author, especially to Tori Bachman, Sharon Wu, Nancy Chung, Amy Schroller, Colleen Brennan, Margaret O'Connor, and Gail Buschman for bringing this book to life, cover to endnotes.

Special thanks for your generosity to Mira McEwan, Irene Latham and Charles Waters, Martín Espada, Janet Wong, James McHale and Kielty Turner, Ariel Francisco, Jeff Zentner, Philip Gross, Gary Soto, Ross Gay, the Robert Lax Literary Trust, Tanya Shadrick, Alex Dimitrov, Kevin Carey, Rose Hauger, and Hayden Saunier for allowing me to republish poetry in this book.

To Karen Lubenetski and Audrey Mathison and Candace Brobst and Karen Blomain and the all of the teachers who helped me grow along the way. To the 2,400+ students through the years who challenged me to keep growing and to the many students and families who granted permission to share a little bit of their excellence in this book. To the

Bucks County Library and its librarians, who gave me access to books and articles I needed to research this book.

To Alyssa Walloff, Corinne Sikora, Michele Myers, Suzanne Dailey, Stephanie Thomas, and Brian Novick for affording me professional development opportunities, support, and an ear to my musings on teaching and learning. To Lisa Levin and Kristy Trammell and Jason Hepler, my supportive PLC teammates and to Kevin Shillingford, my principal.

To Matthew Johnson, Nicholas Emmanuele, and Amy Ludwig VanDerwater for their you-can-do-it attitude when I needed it most.

To all the contributors to the *Go Poems* blog through the years, who helped me to understand what frequent poetry lessons can look like in classrooms around the world.

PUBLISHER'S ACKNOWLEDGMENTS

Corwin gratefully acknowledges the contributions of the following reviewers:

Jim Burke
English Teacher and Author
San Francisco, CA

Andy Schoenborn
English Teacher and Author
Midland, MI

Lyschel Shipp
English Teacher and Author
Buford, GA

Theresa Walter
English Teacher
Greenlawn, NY

Melissa Wood-Glusac
English Teacher
Thousand Oaks, CA

ABOUT THE AUTHOR

Brett Vogelsinger has been teaching English for twenty years and currently teaches ninth-grade students at Holicong Middle School in Bucks County, Pennsylvania. He is a regular contributor at the *Moving Writers* blog (www.movingwriters .org) and has written about teaching and learning for Edutopia, NCTE Verse, and *The New York Times* Learning Network. When not teaching, grading, or writing about such things, you will likely find him spending time with his family, his garden, or his Jenga tower of books he plans to read. You can find him on Twitter @theVogelman or at his website, www.brettvogelsinger.com.

Dedicated to my wife, Nichole.
Living with an English teacher is not for the faint of heart.

INTRODUCTION

Purposeful Poetry Pauses

This is not a book about writing poems but a book to help students grow as practiced and accomplished writers, first in little poetic steps, and afterward in longer pieces in any genre.

When I announce to my classes of ninth graders each September that we are going to begin every class period with a poem, I am usually greeted with wide eyes and a few reluctant groans. The word *poetry*, for students and adults alike, often conjures past experiences that were uncomfortable, unpleasant, or uninviting.

On one hand, we have students, and many teachers, who have been cornered by a Longfellow poem and forced to dissect it frog-style, pulling out each organ of metaphor, each ligament of allusion, pinning them all with labels. The smell of formaldehyde practically filled the room, and students were left with the impression that poems are complicated, dead things designed by the poet to puzzle readers. These are the students with too much practice in "groan-filled packets of figurative language overkill" (Bernabei & Van Prooyen, 2020, p. xii).

On the other hand, some students are asked to bare their soul in a poem, to tap into their inner Sylvia Plath within a forty-five-minute class period, sharing their depth and vulnerability with a randomly assigned partner for feedback. They perceive poetry as threatening in an entirely different way. These students believe that poetry requires some self-revelation that feels deeply uncomfortable in the classroom and may cling to the damaging myth that writing poetry is a spiritual gift that the universe bestows upon some and not others. If a student is not yet comfortable being as candid or exposed as Rachel Wiley or

Rudy Francisco in their beautiful spoken word pieces, can they still be a poet?

To be clear, I do not oppose teaching poetry explication or writing poetry from our deepest personal experiences. I want my students to be able to wrangle with nineteenth-century poems that are not completely understandable on a first read, AND I want students to grow in their ability to express their deepest personal thoughts and feelings in a genre that invites the exploration of inner space. Too often though, when teachers read and write poems in a single, annual unit, we snowball so much into so little time that we intimidate students into disliking poetry. Sharing a Poem of the Day across an entire school year has opened up a variety of forms, voices, cultural perspectives, subgenres, and mentor texts that make poetry integral in my classroom.

Looking back as I begin my twentieth year of teaching English, my biggest regret is that I did not find a way to weave poetry more frequently into my practice during my early years. After a decade of doing this daily, it is hard to imagine any other way. But even if daily poetry exposure is not possible within the structure of the English curriculum where you teach, learning to slip and weave it into the fabric of our instruction through planned, regular poetry pauses can help our writers work with language in fresh, exciting ways that cultivate precision and patience as they craft their words.

POETRY PAUSES DEFINED

What is a poetry pause? Nothing complicated.

It is part of a class period, ranging from three minutes to an entire class period, when we learn in the presence of a poem. Sometimes it involves just giving ear to a beautiful combination of words and noticing something about how those words work. But often it is more. It likely involves some friendly discussion of a poem, some teasing out of its thinking, and a little bit of time writing alongside the poem in our writer's notebook, perhaps imitating one of the writer's craft moves. Many days it stirs some awakening for me, as my students notice facets of the poem that I overlooked. Poetry pauses allow for the frequent, gradual acquisition of skills that students can apply to their longer, more traditional academic writing.

Anyone can lead students to more skilled and precise writing with poetry pauses. I have neither an MFA nor a poetry chapbook to my name. I have always loved words, but that is a trait common among

English teachers. To invite poetry into your practice more often does not require you to be a reader or writer of poetry in your free time (though it may have that side effect), nor must you necessarily consider yourself a creative person. You do not need to be skilled in the surgical art of scansion or explication, though if you are, you can certainly draw upon that background. What it does require is setting aside your own preconceptions about poetry as an esoteric genre, perhaps borne of the same sorts of experiences as a student that I describe in the opening paragraphs of this book.

If we all have favorite songs that sing in our hearts and replay in our minds long after we listen to them with lyrics that stir us and echo through our daily experiences, then we are already poetry lovers, and primed to invite that same kind of heady delight into our classrooms. We simply need press pause now and then to give ourselves the room to do it.

Aside from the two common approaches to poetry described above, there is a third, valuable purpose for working with poems: to invite our students into writing. Interrupting our writing process with poetry pauses to read, explore, and write in our writer's notebooks can help students hone their own craft in all genres. We do not even need to expect that our students write particularly excellent poems to reap these rewards. And when we invite them to write in this genre more often, even if it cannot be daily exposure, their writing work more often crosses the line into excellence.

Ultimately, the writing process, we now acknowledge, is not quite as lockstep and linear as it was when my teachers first introduced it to me as a student in the early 1990s. Most writers do some revision while drafting. We might pause to reevaluate an outline as we revise. We brainstorm multiple ways to express or punctuate a thought as we edit. Neither are the modes of writing quite as clear-cut as we once taught them. Many excellent arguments include a thread of narrative, and an informative piece may include an infographic or other visual component at its core.

Writing requires nimbleness and pausing to write poetry or at least think poetically during assignments for academic classes can help students open new possibilities for their work and help that work to feel a bit more like play. In a 2018 commentary piece in *The Atlantic* called "Poetry Is Everywhere," Megan Garber points out that part of the resurgence of poetry comes from its uncanny ability to blur genre lines, like the "poetry meeting documentary" format of the PBS series *Poetry in America* or Rupi Kaur's enormously popular blend of artwork and short verse on Instagram. Garber writes, "Poetry can't die any more than air or water can meet such an end, because poetry in the more expansive sense is not 'poetry' in the narrow. Poetry is permeative; it is currency; and it is, thankfully, too big to die" (para. 5). This big, permeative nature allows teachers to channel its energy into every type of student writing.

Annesley Anderson, a tutor in a college writing center who works with students across all disciplines, published an article about how helpful short, creative prompts can be to struggling writers. Brief creative writing can become "a tool to disrupt students' preconceived ideas about the writing process and boost writerly agency" (Anderson, 2020, para. 1). Poems provide the kind of healthy disruption a writer may need to filter out a main point from a flood of ideas or sharpen the language around a provocative claim. By shifting the angle from which we approach a writing task, we can help make success more attainable.

Creative pauses as catalysts for thought are not unique to the English classroom. Scientists value them, too. In a column titled "Writing Takes Work," from the journal *Nature*, British geomorphologist Eli Lazarus (2017) notes that "even technical writing is a creative process" and "everyone can benefit from a good writers' workshop" when navigating "the warrens of the writing process" (p. 291). In *Entangled Life*, his marvelously poetic book about fungi, Merlin Sheldrake (2020) affirms that "imagination forms part of the everyday business of inquiry . . . asking questions about a world that was never made to be catalogued and systematized" (p. 20). Expert in scientific communication Dr. Sam Illingworth (2022) suggests that scientific communication fails to reach some audiences because it alienates them up as "non-experts" and that poetry can "break down these barriers," becoming "a conduit between the science and a wider audience" (paras. 7–8). The ability to shift to an imaginative, creative perspective and back again, valued among top scientists, can be nurtured by English teachers who, on a regular basis, pause for a poem.

To understand the potential that poetry has to help our students grow as writers, we will start to examine how infusing poems into our lessons more often can help students learn to think with poetry, feel more comfortable reading and discussing a poem, and notice the craft choices that make writing shine. Then in each subsequent chapter, we will look at how poetry pauses can be helpful to student writers at each stage of the writing process and in various modes of writing.

Along the way, I will share lots of favorite poems and pauses, some longer workshop lessons that help students tap into their creative energy and propel their writing, and some potential pitfalls to avoid.

WHY POETRY?

Daily poetry in the classroom is not a new or revolutionary idea. I first discovered it as an undergraduate student hearing about Billy Collins's poet laureate project, *Poetry 180: A Poem a Day for American High Schools*. The project's concept was simple: read a poem daily with students to increase their exposure to the variety, the linguistic acrobatics, the beauty of poetry, and then do not kill it with commentary and analysis. Nancie Atwell says, "If ever I had to choose just one genre to teach in a middle school English program, it would be poetry. The lessons it teaches kids about good writing, about critical reading, about the kind of adults they wish to become and the kind of world they hope to inhabit, extend the best invitation I can imagine to grow up healthy and whole" (Atwell et al., 2013, n.p.). I am sure this idea was not new in the turn of the twenty-first century, and if I give Billy Collins or Nancie Atwell credit for creating the concept, I am certain a retired teacher from the 1970s will send me an e-mail about how they followed this same routine decades ago.

Teachers know that a simple routine can anchor a class. A close friend and math teacher uses a quote projected on the screen to discuss each day and build community before diving into algebra. Another friend uses a word of the day routine to build vocabulary. These simple brushstrokes can become a teacher's signature on a course, and Poem of the Day has become mine.

Starting this routine, I discovered there was something elemental about poetry. I discovered that nearly everything else I needed to impart about writing well could be tucked into a succinct lesson efficiently and intensely with the help of a poem. And it all started by just welcoming more of this genre into our space, gaining comfort with reading it, listening to it, watching it performed, and writing it.

At present, poetry is experiencing a renaissance and reinvention as poems go viral on Facebook and "Instapoets" blend imagery and brief verse in perfect shareable squares. Patrick Stewart shared Shakespeare sonnet read-alouds with the world during the COVID-19 pandemic and Brandon Leake stole America's heart as the first spoken-word poet to rise to fame on *America's Got Talent*; the *Ours Poetica* series on YouTube brings us famous people's favorite poetry while Terrence

Hayes showed up in an advertisement for Dove and Amanda Gorman made the cover of *Vogue*. There is, as poet Craig Morgan Teicher puts it, "a robust culture of sharing poetry online and young people have taken control of how they consume literature" (as cited in Lund, 2021, para. 15). It makes sense for our classrooms to embrace poetry right now. The world beyond our classrooms has already opened its arms.

What makes poetry so valuable in helping us to teach writers? A few things.

1. **Poems are (often) short.** This means they can demonstrate a key writing skill we want students to apply more efficiently than longer genres. No one feels like they have extra time lying around to try a new strategy, but employing poetry pauses asks for only a few precious minutes of class time with the promise of exponential returns in our students' writing.

2. **Poems are rich.** This means each word counts for more. As Rita Dove puts it, "poetry is language at its most distilled and powerful." Reading and writing poems regularly helps our students tune in to the nuance of individual words. Distilled, powerful language strengthens any piece of writing, not just poetry.

3. **Poems connect to our other reading.** We can often find in poems thematic echoes of the longer works we study in class. This gives us the chance to look at how more than one text handles a topic and perceive varied approaches as we enter "a vast conversation spanning thousands of years" (Teicher, quoted in Lund, 2021, para. 17). It also helps us dovetail reading, writing, speaking, and listening standards in our curriculum.

4. **Poems contain patterns.** Like music, poems rely on rhythm, repetition, and sound to convey ideas. Writing in all sorts of genres is described as "poetic" when a reviewer wants to commend the sound and texture of a writer's work. Working with patterns can help students quickly improve their writing with sound effects to heighten a reader's attention and underscore main ideas and turning points in their work.

5. **Poems engage our neurology in exciting ways.** Researchers now know that after reading poems with metaphors that require particularly bold leaps of the imagination, high school students demonstrate improved fluency and flexibility, important measures of creativity (Osowiecka & Kolanczyk, 2018). We know that poetry can elicit chills and goosebumps, and when these are measured via neuroimaging, they touch our brain's reward centers in ways

that are akin to, but different from, listening to music. Even test subjects unaccustomed to reading poetry experienced these neurological outcomes (Wassiliwizky et al., 2017).

6. **Poems invite diverse voices.** Because of poems' brevity, reading poetry frequently and using poems as mentors make it easy to introduce a wide array of cultures from all around the world over the course of an academic term. For many of my students, Poem of the Day marks their first time reading a piece of literature from South America, Africa, or North America's First Peoples. It embeds work that has been published days or weeks ago. This improves our students' opportunities to learn from some writers who have lived experiences different from their own.

For seven years, I have been writing and publishing brief pieces about the value that frequent work with poetry adds to an English class. In 2016, I started an annual blogging project for National Poetry Month in the United States called *Go Poems* and invited teachers from throughout North America to join me. The project highlights how short poetry pauses can provide portals to deeper thinking and writing with secondary students from any grade level. Curating posts from colleagues gave me the opportunity to learn what poetry pauses can look like in schools in Newark (NJ) and Edmond (OK), Dallas and Ontario, in urban schools, rural schools, and in each region of the continent with students from diverse backgrounds. It has been heartening to notice the common threads listed earlier and the ease and enthusiasm with which teachers are introducing this simple practice into their classrooms.

Scan this QR code to check out my Go Poems project that ran from 2016-2022.

We are all busy, working through overstuffed curriculum, demanding standards, and inflexible schedules for standardized tests which have, in some cases, removed poetry from the eligible content. But when something offers us an influence that radiates through *everything* students write, not just an impactful lesson for an assignment or a particular genre, it is worth the relatively narrow investment of time.

Try opening little nooks of space for poetry, daily if possible. For the first week or two share a different poem each day. Choose poems so short that you can read them or listen to them out loud twice in five minutes. Many potent poems are so short that two readings take less time than five minutes! I am thrilled to share and exemplify the impact that pausing for poems has had on my classroom and my student writers, and I hope you will find many ideas to apply within these pages.

GETTING STARTED WITH POETRY PAUSES

Typically, my first Poem of the Day each year is "Invitation," the opening poem from Shel Silverstein's *Where the Sidewalk Ends* (1974). I choose this poem for a few reasons. Both my ninth-grade students and I have some positive childhood interactions with Silverstein's poetry. This memorable book reminds us that poems can be whimsical and fun, dark-but-light all at once, and that poetry books can be page-turners. I share with my students that I do not remember this particular poem from childhood, but approaching it as an older reader, I notice some things that I would never have found interesting in third grade when I first encountered this book.

After the first read-aloud and before our second reading, I invite students to notice anything that jumps out at them as an older reader in ninth grade that they think they would have overlooked as a younger reader. What do they see now that they could not really "see" before? Since it is the first day, some classes start slowly. But if needed, I start to ask some follow-up questions like "What words are most interesting here? Do you notice any punctuation you would not have noticed as a younger reader? What does this line about 'magic bean buyers' or this one about 'flax-golden tales to spin' refer to?" Noticing these allusions to Jack and the Beanstalk and Rumpelstiltskin in the poem opens their eyes to what they may have missed at a younger age, even though we do not use the word *allusion* in this opening lesson.

Within the first several weeks, I have students wondering about the line in Mary Oliver's "At Blackwater Pond" that says water "tastes/like stone, leaves, fire." We discuss, "Which of those words is most interesting and why?" We get talking about our childhood reactions to thunder after reading Jean Toomer's "Storm Ending," which begins with the lines "Thunder blossoms gorgeously above our heads/ Great, hollow, bell-like flowers." We talk about how poets find the magical in the mundane in the poem "What the Window Washers Did" by Margaret Hasse and pick out words that make the act of washing a window sound like an act of magic in that poem.

The early part of the year is about setting the tone and learning to think with poetry. There is no secret recipe for what poems to share or what to tease out of them.

The critical skill to develop early in the year is comfort and intrigue with what poems have to say and how they say it. Carol Jago (2019) describes the necessary balance we bring to poetry beautifully in *The Book in Question*:

> Too much teaching and students are intimidated; too little and they are lost. I want students to hold a poem in their hands the way they [hold a] precious object, to feel a poem's beauty before worrying about what it means. I don't want them putting gold frames around poems with the label "Great Art" but rather to see for themselves by looking closely, carefully, lovingly at what is there to behold. (p. 83)

When students develop the skill of seeing poems for themselves and approaching poetry in the manner Jago describes, they are not just developing as readers but as writers, too. I might even extend Jago's metaphor. Student writers can learn to handle poems like beautiful objects made of clay that have not yet been in the kiln, that are published, but not fixed, still malleable in their hands to play with and learn from in their notebooks by pinching and reshaping and reimagining the poems with their own artistic touches.

Now, a caveat: my students right now are the oldest students in their Grades 7-9 building. They have had some exposure to poetry earlier in their academic lives in this school and have kept writer's notebooks before. In general, a reading and writing workshop format is comfortable to them. They come to class with a measure of confidence, even though their experience with reading and writing poetry will be much deeper and vaster by June. So if these examples sound a little pie-in-the-sky for your students as you first meet them, alter the ideas in this book in a way that works for you, and that will open room for comfortable poetry writing later in the year.

You might try quick visualization exercises: "Close your eyes while I read this poem. What images stand out to you after hearing it?" Then the following day, "After our second reading of this poem, turn it into a two-minute sketch in your writer's notebook. Talk about your sketching decisions with a partner. What details did you decide to include?" In a 1-to-1 environment, use a quick, collaborative mood board on Pear Deck for each day of that first week, asking, "How does this poem leave you feeling?" Our goal at the start of the year is to help students hold the clay in their hands and get comfortable with it so that they can later mold it into something of their own.

When it feels right, or when an inquisitive student raises a hand to ask a question, start inviting students to share more and more of what they notice. Pause and ask yourself this, too (what do *you* notice?), and tune in to how much more you are able to notice over the course of just a short two-week period. Likely, when visiting an art museum, you do not notice much in the first few paintings. Your mind is still racing from the world outside. The silence inside the museum has not yet seized you. But a gallery or two later, your eyes are opening, and the details become more inviting and intriguing. The same thing happens with poems.

Reading and writing poetry regularly as a class strips away some of our teacher fears. The habit allows us to discover poets we were not taught in high school or college, living poets from around the world whose playfulness and inventiveness with language is totally different than anything we have read before. It introduces us to ideas and perspectives well outside the field of canonical English literature: works in translation, marginalized voices. Poetry pushes us as teachers, and it beckons us to write more, too.

The chart below outlines some noble goals that we might seek to achieve within the first six weeks of school to help us deploy the power of poetry in our writing process later in the year. These goals help us establish poetry as a foundation for our thinking in class rather than as a decoration. The methods and timing you choose to meet these goals may vary depending on your students' level of enthusiasm for learning and apprehension about poetry. The chart is not meant to be in any way prescriptive, because the best work with poetry will always be the product of the community and curiosity you build with the students before you.

Week	Goal	Possible Methods	Possible Questions and Prompts
1-2	Getting comfortable listening to poetry	1. Listening to poems 2. Watching videos of spoken-word poems 3. Talking about broad impressions of poems 4. Noticing what fascinates or affects us in poems	What do you like about this poem? What bugs you about it? What is the most interesting line here? What would you ask the writer of this poem? How does this poem leave you feeling?
3-4	Noticing details in poems	1. Listening for sound effects in poems 2. Noticing delivery style in spoken-word poems 3. Talking about our taste in poems 4. Noticing shifts and changes in poems	What word combinations sound cool together in this poem? What does the poet do in performing this poem to add power? What is your favorite word or phrase in this poem? How does this poem move or change from the beginning to the end of it?

Week	Goal	Possible Methods	Possible Questions and Prompts
5	Noticing the poet's choices in a poem	1. Listening for artful word choice 2. Noticing punctuation, line breaks, stanzas, pauses 3. Talking about the power of words 4. Noticing how our understanding changes with a second reading	What is special about this word or phrase in the poem? What does it make you think about? What is the most important pause or break in this poem? Which line is still ringing in your head when the poem ends? What do you notice on a second reading that you missed the first time? What questions does that provoke?
6	Using poems as mentors for our own expression	1. Listening for things you would like to learn to do as a writer 2. Noticing patterns we can try to replicate 3. Talking about specific devices and diction the writer is using and possible reasons for those devices 4. Noticing what the writer is choosing NOT to do, say, or explain	Which parts of this poem make you jealous as a writer: "I want to write like that!" What is happening here in the poem? Let's try a line (or stanza) like that in our notebooks. Why is this metaphor fitting for this topic? What are the connotations of this word? Why did the writer choose to do X, not Y? What makes this choice the best possible for this poem?

For poetry to be useful to students as writers of a wide array of genres, it must be approachable to them as readers. They must develop an ear for it, an eye for it, and a comfort with it. Investing a little time in lots of poetic exposure early in the year allows students to make lots of their own poetry in fairly little time later in the year—poetry that contributes to the successful writing process of all different genres, modes, and forms.

Like any teacher, I cannot say that every lesson or unit successfully tugs at the wonder of every student's heart. But I can say with confidence by the end of the year, I have won over even the naysayers and eye-rollers of September with Poem of the Day. Every student leaves with some poems that are lasting, bonded memories. Students look forward to this signature element, this few-minutes-long-and-sometimes-longer routine that propels us into each day's lesson and allows us to welcome viewpoints from across the continents and the centuries into our little space to learn together. The small, gemlike quality of poems makes this possible. The conversations they spark, the "tune-ups" of our noticing skills, and the introductions to longer lessons these poems provide are invaluable.

Do not let the perception that "my students just are not into poetry" stop you from trying a more frequent integration of the genre. Remember that they have likely been conditioned through tightly controlled, once-a-year experiences to feel this way. When we have narrow exposure to something, it is hard to fall in love with it. So if you struggle with this perception, or a class who is bold about vocalizing their disdain for the genre, assure them that what you are doing is different than their past experiences with poems. The poems will be varied, and so will the purposes for reading them.

Increasing exposure to poetry helps students feel more comfortable and fluent in all sorts of writing. Crafting a poem no longer scares them and is no longer synonymous with having to drum up a Seussian rhythm and rhyme, as they may have grown accustomed to doing in elementary school. Taking time to think through poetry helps us to see poetry as a fertile garden for thinking, and soon those writer's notebook poems we tinker with are helping us craft better essays, reviews, and research papers. As we wander through the lines, we wonder in our minds. This habit of mind not only cultivates close and insightful reading but also facilitates the nimble, poetic writing that can help us quickly practice and apply key writing skills that transfer to any genre.

How to Find Poems

My most frequently asked question when I start to share my enthusiasm for poetry in teacher workshops is "How? How do you find all the poems you share with your students?" So often in teaching we know that things are harder than they look. This is not the case with finding excellent, approachable poems. It is *easier* than it looks. Here are my suggestions:

1. **Sign up for daily poetry e-mails.** The *Writer's Almanac*, Poets.org, and *The Slowdown* podcast e-mails have provided me with the bulk of my favorite poems for class, in a daily, manageable drip.

2. **Follow #TeachLivingPoets on Twitter.** A devoted group of teachers will introduce you to an ever-expanding online library from living poets with an emphasis on social justice. Find new voices, professional connections, and chats about contemporary poems.

3. **Explore *Poetry 180*.** Though it is almost 20 years old, this compendium is still available for free on the Library of Congress website and provides a poem a day for the whole school year. Two poetry anthologies have been published under the Poetry 180 moniker as well, so if you need a cheat sheet, a few are waiting for you.

4. **Browse the stacks.** Visit your local bookstore or library and pull books from the poetry section. Flip through and find the poets who are accessible on the first reading and get even better on the second reading.

5. **Get involved in National Poetry Month projects.** The Geraldine Dodge Poetry Foundation, NCTE, and Poetry Foundation each have their own!

6. **Borrow and buy collections of children's poetry.** If you have young children in your family, read them aloud to them. If not, read them to yourself. These poems have the same beauty as poems written for an older audience and will give you the warm-up you need to come home to this genre. Get to know the work of Irene Latham and Charles Waters, Amy Ludwig VanDerwater, Georgia Heard, Lee Bennet Hopkins, Janet Wong, and Anna Grossnickle Hines.

7. **Visit this book's companion website.** It transforms all written lists from the print edition into link libraries to help you easily find poems listed in this book that are published online.

HOW TO CHOOSE POEMS

When choosing which poems to incorporate in my Poem of the Day routine, I try to keep a few things in mind. I am careful to diversify the voices from what my students come across in their standard curriculum. It is also an important opportunity to demonstrate how hospitable poetry can be, so I want poems that are at least somewhat accessible on a first reading. Like great movies, the best poems to choose will give me something else to notice on subsequent readings.

I try to choose poems that will not perpetuate the myth that poetry is esoteric, dark, and subtly condescending. Billy Collins once told me that he thinks part of the reason his poems speak so broadly to readers is that they are not "conveyor belts of misery," so I remember that poetry pauses can sometimes grant students a needed emotional break from the heavier themes we discuss in class. I want poems that feel fresh and vivid and are economical with words. The poems I choose should strike me as interesting and inspiring, because I know my enthusiasm and wonder have the potential to be contagious.

None of this is a result of any special gift of mine. These facets of poetry that I embrace and share are gifts of the genre itself. When we carve out time for poetry pauses, we interrupt the flow of our day in a good way and often a way that moves us to write. For me, that pause works in the beginning of class each day. This book reveals that poetry pauses can provide intentional interruption to our writing process, new lenses to our writing modes, and fresh energy to our competency as writers.

Do not feel that you need to have a daily routine or a 180-slide PowerPoint presentation in place to start using poetry for the purposes described in this book. You might choose to go there, and you might not. You might include a Poetry Friday routine (Wong & Vardell, 2017), or you might work with colleagues in a professional learning community to curate a collection of poems from contemporary voices that you wish to weave into your regularly scheduled units this year. What I can tell you with confidence is that a more integrated, regular routine of poetry reading and writing will open up doors for the young writers beside you. It will coax you into a bolder writing process as well. I feel comfortable guaranteeing that. It is your money-back guarantee on this book.

This book does not argue that increased exposure to poetry makes better writers, even though there is probably truth in that. It reveals that poetry can be the heartbeat of a class that keeps the lifeblood flowing through all of our students' compositions. It shakes us from the misconception that poetry should be confined to an annual unit of study and instead shows how it can bring life to *every* unit. This is not a book about writing poems, but a book to help students grow as practiced and accomplished writers, first in little poetic steps, and afterward in longer pieces in any genre.

Here I share twenty of my all-time favorite poems to share with my ninth-grade students, many of them linked on this book's companion website. I hope you might find a few to enjoy and share with your class as well. But more than this, I hope you use the tools in this chapter to collect your own set of favorites and cultivate a classroom where thinking grows through poetry, to find poems that nourish the student writers before you and prepare them for the growth and community that await them in writing workshops throughout the year.

Twenty of My All-Time Favorite Poems to Share With Students

1. "Famous" by Naomi Shihab Nye

2. "Quilts" by Nikki Giovanni

3. "Revenge" by Taha Muhammad Ali

4. "Pass On" by Michael Lee (spoken word)

5. "Complainers" by Rudy Francisco (spoken word)

6. "Swift Things Are Beautiful" by Elizabeth Coatsworth

7. "Camaro" by Phil Kaye (spoken word)

8. "Absolute" by Jacqueline Woodson

9. "Dawn, Revisited" by Rita Dove

10. "The Arm" by Stephen Dunn

11. "At Blackwater Pond" by Mary Oliver

12. "Snow Day" by Billy Collins

13. "Poem Written in the Parking Lot of a Tattoo Shop While Waiting for an Appointment" by Ariel Francisco

14. "Turkey Vultures" by Michael Collier

15. "testify" by Eve L. Ewing

16. "We Wear the Mask" by Paul Laurence Dunbar

17. "Remember" by Joy Harjo

18. "Alley Violinist" by Robert Lax

19. "In Two Seconds" by Mark Doty

20. "The Human Family" by Maya Angelou

HOW TO USE THIS BOOK, THE APPENDICES, AND THE COMPANION WEBSITE

The seven chapters in this book cover a whole range of ideas pertaining to the writing process and writing products. It was my goal to organize this book so that no matter the project, genre, or step in the writing process your class is working on, it is possible to find a poetry pause that is helpful.

Each chapter has some subheadings that share research and rationale behind the ideas and some subheadings that begin with the words "Poetry Pause" followed by a quick, spotlighted overview of what an activity looks like in class before taking you on a deeper dive.

When you need to modify an idea in this book by either streamlining it or scaffolding it, refer to Appendix A, full of best practices you can use. Occasionally, sidebars will direct you to a particular streamlining or scaffolding method that I think is a good fit for a specific lesson.

Additionally, some lessons have reproducible handouts you may find useful. These can be photocopied from Appendix B or printed from the ancillary resources for this book on its companion website.

Scan this QR code to access the companion website and links to the poems that are listed in this book.

There are numerous lists of poems within this book. The book's companion website has these lists digitized by chapter, so with each list, you have a ready set of links! If you prefer, a quick search of the title and poet is often all it takes to have a poem mentioned in this book right beside you as you think through the suggested activities, and the QR codes you will find throughout this book further streamline this process. In fact, here is a QR code to take you right to the companion website!

The companion website also contains some additional ideas I have added to the book post-publication that you can share with colleagues to pique their interest in this method.

As you read this book, it is possible you will find ideas that feel inviting but also intimidating to use with your students. You know your students the best, and no two teachers deliver instruction in the same way. Teachers are expert craftspeople, not robots. As you unpack the full knapsack of ideas here in your class, I trust you completely. Modify what you find here and make it your own.

IT ALL COMES DOWN TO THIS

Writing can be enjoyable, and teaching writing can be difficult.

Poetry pauses can enhance our joy, and they can help make teaching writing a little easier.

I hope that you will find the practices in this book as nourishing to you and your students as I have found them for me and for mine. I hope your students' writer's notebooks light up with better words than ever before, and I hope they feel proud to transfer those skills from poems to all the other genres you explore.

Researcher Ismael Baroudy (2008) writes that "most successful student-writers are almost consciously or unconsciously process-writing fans." They are "multiple-drafters, recursive-thinkers, meaning-seekers, form-neglectors, quick-writers, feedback-anticipators" and "journal keepers" (para. 25). Poetry pauses draw out and celebrate this kind of realistic creative practice.

Poetry pauses keep me learning, engaged, and creating alongside my students. I hope they will do that for you, too. As you collect the poems and practices that work best in your world, I hope you will pass what you learn to others and back to me. Together, we will keep on growing.

1

POETRY TO BRING ON THE BRAINSTORM

When we invite students to brainstorm, we are asking them to open up and welcome new ideas. The word itself implies a downpour, a deluge of ideas, an opening wide of the heavens with dramatic thunder and lightning. In the best-case scenario, I picture a writer standing in the rain, face upturned and eyes closed, getting soaked with a torrent of possibilities.

Mrs. Lubenetski, my second-grade teacher, was a star at getting good brainstorms out of the class. With a wide smile, a snappy, electrified voice, and a 1989 perm, she circulated the room, gesturing and laughing and generating palpable excitement for our wild imaginings. There were endless stacks of paper to use. There were no wrong answers. There were not even iffy answers. The completely unfiltered nature of a good brainstorm was refreshing to me at age seven. Opportunities seemed endless.

Strangely, I have fewer memories of really good brainstorms as a teenager, and now that I teach secondary students, I realize this may have something to do with how teens quickly and severely edit themselves to avoid embarrassment. The best brainstorms ignore the possibility of embarrassment and favor the promise of discovery.

For instance, I remember that in a quest to introduce greater choice into my writing workshops, instead of giving my students a list of possible topics for argument writing, I asked them to brainstorm.

"Write a list of everything you care about, everything that gets you riled up in the world, everything you want to change!" I enthused. "I'll set the timer for five minutes, and when we're finished, we'll pick one of these ideas we'd like to turn into an essay."

A "braindrizzle" ensued, ideas trickling onto paper while I tried to conduct frenzied, lightning-rod conferences around the room during the five-minute time limit.

There was no storm.

How can poems help to address this phenomenon? And how can poetry writing produce the generative thinking that prepares our students for other writing?

Brainstorming and poetry writing have a few essential elements in common:

1. **Creative Imagination:** Brainstorming is a creative act. It is not a big stretch to suppose that some creative writing can help a student initiate any writing task. Poet Ted Hughes, in the preface to his book *Poetry Is* (1970), says that "by showing to a pupil's imagination many opportunities and few restraints, and instilling into him confidence and a natural motive for writing, the odds are that something . . . of our common genius will begin to put a word in" (p. xvii). These are the same conditions we hope to offer students at the beginning of their writing process when they stir up ideas. While his words are about teaching young people to write poetry, the same principles apply to teaching them about writing in any genre.

2. **Poignant Focus:** As Linda Rief says in her introduction to *The Quickwrite Handbook* (2018), "helping students find a way to get their initial ideas on paper helps them build confidence to realize that they do have something to say. When the writing is so focused, so detailed, and so poignant so quickly, it gives them a solid direction for expanding on that idea" (p. 3). Poetry mentor texts are focused, detailed, and poignant. I love how students can read a poem they have never seen before, notice a pattern, and use it as a guide to write one that echoes it in their writer's notebook.

   Often, both the student and I stand back and smile at just how beautiful their thinking sounds in just a short sweep of time! This inspires them to keep going, firing up their motivation to move on to drafting. Most importantly, a poetry pause that we invest *before* our students start thinking about pages and paragraphs, word count, rubrics, and form helps them focus on the *heart* of their work before they focus on what is measured or assessed. How much have we choked out brainstorming capabilities by frontloading our student assignments with assessment and grading details?

3. **Freedom:** Poet Craig Morgan Teicher (2018) notes that "when poems are working, they are full of discoveries, thoughts poets didn't know they had, thoughts, perhaps, they hadn't had until that moment" (pp. 4-5). When our students write, we want them to recover, uncover, and discover not only ideas that excite them but also the words to express those ideas. Former poet laureate Robert Pinsky begins his book *Singing School* (2014) with a whole section called "Freedom" about the artistic inventiveness poets relish. He opens with the words "There are no rules." For poets, "impulses, swerves, collisions, flights, descents, gags, indirections, surprises, exploding cigars, non sequiturs: all are allowed or encouraged" (p. 3) This list describes the elementary school giddiness we strive to help our adolescent brainstormers recapture, but it comes from a description written for adult poets. This is an intersection worth visiting.

As I have learned to approach brainstorms poetically, it has changed everything I say about writing assignments, which means I can eliminate the off-putting pressure that my words about the scope of an assignment or its grading previously imposed when students were just beginning. Instead, my students and I are jumping into our writer's notebooks, harnessing the energy we have, and generating more voluminous ideas as we craft a verse.

BRAINSTORMING WITH POETRY: STEP BY STEP

When you plan to use a poem to initiate a brainstorm, it is worth thinking through a few questions.

1. **What kind of ideas do you want?** We know that some ideas students generate will be better than others. For example, for a personal narrative, accounts of family vacations do not tend to be riveting. The only one of those I can really remember years after reading it was the story of a family who got caught with one tire of their rental car hanging over a cliff, and that was more a survival story than a vacation play-by-play. So my first move when I try to decide how poetry can help with a brainstorm is to find a poem that steers students away from the common pitfalls like

those dry travelogues that open with a drive to the airport. Some of the ideas in this chapter are best for finding a topic. Others are good for brainstorming content to develop a topic.

2. **What kind of poem will provoke those kinds of ideas?** To continue the personal narrative example, the perfect poem to help students brainstorm would be one that presents a series of moments in just a few words with pops of vivid imagery. Of course, there is no easy way to google such a poem, so I keep my eyes peeled using the daily poetry e-mail resources and podcasts I wrote about in the introduction. Poems that feel like photo albums or home videos or flipbooks start to catch my eye: these poems invite brainstorms for narrative writing. When I come across poems that I think will help with this type of brainstorm, I may file them in an e-mail folder labeled "Brainstorm Poems" or add them to my ever-expanding PowerPoint for Poems of the Day. Each year, I organize that PowerPoint roughly by unit so that I have a section of poems that fit nicely into mini-lessons for our personal narrative writing already snowballed together and stored digitally in one place.

3. **How will you point out the pattern?** If you have a Poem of the Day routine, this may be as simple as sharing the poem and asking your students, "What pattern holds this poem together? What makes it tick?" If you are short on time, or it is early in the year, or your students do not feel comfortable with reading like a writer quite yet, you may just point out, "Hey, the first thing that strikes me about this poem is the way it kind of firecrackers out, like an explosion of ideas. Do you see that too? It's like one idea strikes the writer, and then that one sparks another and another and the whole poem kind of sizzles after a while."

4. **"Wouldn't it be fun to write like that?"** Use those words to invite students to write a poem that parallels the mentor text. Let them see *you* get excited about the energy of a good storm that exists in the original poem, and let them see *you* try to re-create that frenetic energy too. Write beside it under the document camera and show students what a poem that echoes the mentor poem, written in the moment, might look and sound like. Let students share with a partner or the whole class. Celebrate the wildest imaginations in the room and coax the more guarded ones. Laugh with your students. If you can turn this writing exercise into an impromptu poetry reading, students get to hear each other's ideas, and this tends to spark more of their own. You might start to hear students say, "Oh, yeah, I love that too!"

5. **Revisit the poem as a brainstorm.** It is OK to leave the poems your students write in their notebooks for a day and come back to them the next. And it is also OK to dive right in and say, "Now, no matter what your poem sounds like, there are some really cool ideas hiding out in there. Let's find one, just one, that is worth writing about a little more in a different form." Your students are on their way to a major writing assignment, but they feel like they have just uncovered a tiny piece of what Keats would call "a thing of beauty . . . a joy forever."

There are a few broad categories of mentor poems and poetry pause activities that lend themselves nicely to bringing on the brainstorm. Let's consider them now!

POETRY PAUSE: MAKING A LIST

Poem: "Words That Make My Stomach Plummet" by Mira McEwan

Plan: Students create a list poem, using a mentor text and borrowing its title.

Big Picture: Writing a list poem is a disarming way to brainstorm ideas for an argument essay that requires students to take a stand. Because there is a touch of snarky humor in the original, students are more willing to engage and offer a list of topics they are passionate enough to write more about.

One of the most natural forms for a brainstorm to take is a list. List poems can be incredibly helpful for generating possible topics for writing or for fleshing out details to bring a topic to life.

Published poems-as-lists abound and are easy to find. Mira McEwan's funny-but-oh-so-serious poem, "Words That Make My Stomach Plummet" helps students start to rumble about what irks them in this world—which gets at what they care most about—while also bypassing some of the obstacles to a good brainstorm that teens might encounter. It is perfect for brainstorming argument topics, a replacement for my former "What are you passionate about?" prompt.

First, we read the poem as our Poem of the Day. Like most days, I project the poem on our classroom whiteboard so that all students can see it. This particular poem is accessible from *The Writer's Almanac* website and small enough to print multiple copies on a page, cut them out, and have students tape a copy on the top half of their writer's notebook page.

I say, "In this poem, the poet has gathered a list of all the words and phrases that make her 'stomach plummet.' What do you think that phrase means?" Students can quickly identify with that sick drop that happens in our gut when we hear words we dread, words that we associate with negative life experiences.

Before our second reading, when I invite a student to read this poem aloud, I ask the class to consider this question: "What can you tell me about the speaker in this poem? How can we use our inference skills to learn about this person's life?"

WORDS THAT MAKE MY STOMACH PLUMMET

by Mira McEwan

Committee Meeting.   Burden of Proof.
            The Simple Truth.   Trying To Be Nice.
Honestly. I Could Have Died.   I Almost Cried.
            It's Only a Cold Sore.
      It's My Night.   Trust Me.   Dead Serious.
I Have Everything All Under Control.
            I'm Famous For My Honesty.
      I'm Simply Beside Myself.   We're On The Same Page.
            Let's Not Reinvent The Wheel.
For The Time Being. There Is That.
            I'm Not Just Saying That.
      I Just Couldn't Help Myself.   I Mean It.

Reprinted with permission of the poet. From the book *Ecstatic*. Allbooks, © 2007

If you have been teaching for a while, you know that the same questions land differently in different classes. In some groups, the observations flow freely.

"I don't think this person likes drama," a student volunteers.

"Why is that?" I ask. "What lines clue you in about that?"

"When people say 'I almost cried' or 'I'm simply beside myself,' they are usually being super dramatic."

"And how do we know the speaker in the poem doesn't like that?" I press.

"Because those words make her stomach plummet. They make her sick inside."

"Great observations!"

Another thread students should be able to pull from this poem is that the speaker has trouble trusting other people. Perhaps the speaker has been hurt before. If that observation is not rising to the surface, I might say, "Hmmm. I see phrases like 'Trust me . . . I'm famous for my honesty . . . I mean it.' If those words make someone a little sick inside, what might that show about their life and about their experiences? What might they struggle with?"

Two readings and a brief discussion may take only a few minutes of class time, and notice that there has been no mention of an essay to write. In the back of my mind though, I aim to help my students brainstorm some points of personal passion that they might enjoy writing about. So I ask them to take the next five minutes and write a poem with the same title as this one, using the original as a mentor text: "What words or phrases make your stomach plummet? No need to say why, just write for five minutes, unguarded and honestly, about words and phrases that have this effect on you."

In almost every case, I write along with my students in my own notebook, sometimes under the document camera and sometimes privately. Penny Kittle (2008) has put into words what countless English teachers have discovered: "You really can't teach writing well unless you write yourself. . . . We don't learn many things well just by following directions. We have to ride together."

After writing, I may invite a few students to share with the class, but I do not require this or pressure students to do so. Instead, students can ask the same question about the speaker in the poem, and this time the speaker is themselves. They can circle ideas in their own poem that they find worth writing about. We consider, "What can a reader tell about the speaker in *your* poem?"

For example, if a student included "You're grounded!" and "In-School Suspension" as part of their list poem, what does this reveal? Certainly something different from the student who includes "Cancel Culture" and "TikTok star" in their list. But for both students, a brainstorm for the argument essay has already started, and they are beginning to "take a stand." The students have uncovered some of what bugs them most in the world, "topics of personal passion," without the pressure that phrase might create for them. So while the first student may end up writing about the injustices of the ISS system in the school, the second student may argue that our culture gives attention in harmful ways that narrow our attention and our ability to think deeply.

The more poetry you read, the more list poems you will stumble upon. Collect them. Make a list of list poems! Poets teach us the many ways lists can look and sound and open possibilities. Brainstorms can be just as creative, energizing, and varied. Each one can offer a mentor for short poems that double as brainstorms for the various writing purposes and writing projects that are already in your curriculum.

Other List Poems to Bring on the Brainstorm

Brainstorming Purpose	List Poem Possibility
Imagine a better future; ways to resolve a problem	"The Conditional" by Ada Limón
Thinking through a process; examining parts of a whole	"How to Be Alone" by Tanya Davis
Illuminating or interrogating a problem in society	"Bulletproof Teen" by Katie Houde
Setting the scene for a narrative	"Family Reunion" by Rita Dove
Generating metaphors for more creative imagery	"My Mother's Collander" by Dorianne Laux
Reflecting on wisdom gained through life experiences	"Remember" by Joy Harjo
Bringing humor into the tone of our writing	"Did I Miss Anything?" by Tom Wayman
Evaluating our own preferences; finding a topic for analysis	"What I Like and Don't Like" by Philip Schultz
Gathering vivid vocabulary around a topic	"The Museum of Stones" by Carolyn Forché

POETRY PAUSE: STARTING AN ABECEDARIAN

Poem: "Words for a Better World" by Irene Latham and Charles Waters

Plan: Students create an abecedarian poem about a topic of interest, beginning each line with the next letter of the alphabet.

Big Picture: Abecedarian poems push us to keep going, generating a lot of content quickly around a topic. This allows students to reflect on what raw material may be worthy of more attention and for teachers to confer with them and assist in these writerly decisions.

In September 2020, like so many other teachers around the country, I began the school year with a fully virtual model, meeting new students through a screen instead of face-to-face. This was uncharted territory that made me feel like a first-year teacher all over again, adapting the kind of "getting-to-know-you" work from the first week to an environment that kept us literally, and emotionally, distant from each other.

One routine I was keen to continue through those strange opening days was the Poem of the Day. I trusted poetry to do its thing and tug at our hearts and minds like it always does. I knew that poems would be essential to draw my students closer to me and to draw them closer together, and it gave us, over the course of our opening week, three short reading experiences in common even as we each logged in from a different room to "show up" for English class.

Over the summer, I had read Irene Latham and Charles Waters's beautiful poetry collection for children, *Dictionary for a Better World* (2020). This gem examines an alphabetized range of human emotional assets from Acceptance to Zest, pairing each poem with a brief reflection or anecdote from one of the poets to show what these words look like in action. These reflections often reveal what it looks like to stumble in a situation, to mess up and set things right again. Each page feels like a social and emotional learning (SEL) lesson in a carefully crafted package, waiting to be unwrapped with your students.

The poems also run the gamut of poetic forms from haiku to sestina to limerick to ghazal. These terms are defined on the bottom of each page, so the collection provides a tour of the expansive variety of verse that teachers can use as mentor texts for their students.

The opening poem in the collection is an abecedarian, a twenty-six line poem in which each line begins with the next letter of the alphabet. It is called "Words for a Better World" and it begins like this:

EXCERPT FROM "WORDS FOR A BETTER WORLD"

by Irene Latham and Charles Waters

Awash in attempts to help cool our fevered world, we
Begin simply with words. We savor syllables,
Consider history and meaning. We forge ahead with
Determination, trying to do what's right, though
Each step is filled with uncertainty.

This book is about the power of words and how we use them in life to improve the world, both our own microcosm and the great wide world beyond. The opening abecedarian mines those big, broad, abstract ideas in a way that feels concrete and illuminating.

I shared this poem via a screen-shared photograph of the poem in our videoconferencing so my students could follow along on their laptops as I read the poem aloud. Many times in this book I refer to reading the poems aloud a second time, often inviting a student voice for the second read, but on this day, we only read the poem aloud once. It is a bit longer, our class periods had been shortened for virtual learning, and our primary purpose was to notice how the writers employed the abecedarian form to crack open an idea, to mull it over and investigate it. It's as if the poem is saying: "Can words really change this crazy world? Let's take twenty-six lines and think about that."

A published poem has, of course, been through rounds of revision, but in a rougher form, abecedarians can help writing students accomplish a similar purpose.

So I said to my students, "What I love about this poem is how it muses on a topic. It slows down and lets us see what the poets are thinking about. It almost feels like we are thinking right there with them, right? Like we are joining them in saying, 'This world is crazy and sometimes makes us feel powerless to change it. But maybe, just maybe, we can use words to make a difference. Words can help us to keep ourselves afloat and cast a life preserver to others as well.' The poem works as an invitation to go explore that idea deeper with the poets."

Then I said, "Let's try that today, just on a tiny scale. Write A, B, C to start three lines in your writer's notebooks. Write about your day today and how it's going. Let's take just two minutes and try this." I invited students to share their quick thinking in the chat feature of our videoconference.

Mackenzie included her twin sister in her poem:

> About to be late for school
> Because I woke up too late.
> Caitlyn forgot to set the alarm.

The three-line goal was approachable for day three of school. On Friday, when I had students write to me briefly about their most memorable learning from the first week of full-virtual school, the abecedarian kept coming up in their responses. Many seemed intrigued by this poetic form they had never heard of before. It is a logical step up from the acrostic poems they write throughout their elementary years.

I require students to fill at least three pages in their writer's notebooks each week, some with exercises from class, some with free-choice writing. On our second week of school, I suggested they might try writing a full abecedarian. "First," I told them, "since it's twenty-six lines long, it guarantees you a full page in your notebook. But more importantly, this kind of poem can work as a kind of brainstorm around an idea or concept, something you come back to later when we need an idea for an essay, an argument, a story, or a research topic." What I was getting at, but did not articulate just yet, is that this type of poem could help them break down their filter, write past the obvious, and already start to swirl some content around a topic of their choice that interested them.

I found Rosaleen to be a quieter student during those first few weeks of school, an attentive listener on our videoconference class periods but not a frequent participant in class discussion. When I asked students on week three to share any abecedarian poems they had written as part of their free choice writing, I was thrilled to see an e-mail from her pop up in my inbox. She shared her poem "Nature," and I am happy to have her permission to share that rough draft here:

NATURE

After the winter comes all kinds of wild life grows like
Beautiful flowers growing big and tall and little bees buzz-
    ing around,
Caterpillars turning into incredible butterflies that fly for the
    first time
Ducks finally swimming gracefully in ponds after the winter.
Eagles fly high up in the sky and zoom down to get food.
Frogs jumping from lily pad to lily pad while getting bugs
Grasshoppers hopping on tall grass making loud noises
Hummingbirds come out and sing their little songs
Insects come out and eat leaves, seeds, and wood
Jackrabbits hop along for the first time after winter
Koalas playing on the trees jumping from one to another
    eating leaves
Ladybugs crawling everywhere on trees and windows
Mice running around in the grass trying to find food or cheese
Newts crawling on the ground repairing their broken and
    damaged limbs
Owls spying at night for mice and other tasty things they like
Pelicans soaring on water to catch a fish to eat
Qinling pandas walking around with giant steps

Red foxes coming out to explore nature and find more food

Snakes, crawling on their bellies, slithering around everywhere

Turtles slowly crossing the street, trying to save themselves from cars

Urchins, black in color, with claw-like structures on their bodies.

Vampire bats living in dark cold places like caves

Whales, the largest animals on earth, swimming around
catching fish

X-ray fish swimming around finding insects to feed on

Yellow mongoose, living in grasslands and scrublands with
their burrows

Zebras with their black and white stripes to keep bugs away.

I can tell from her poem that Rosaleen loves animals and notices the details of their behavior. I wonder if she has a future mapped out as a veterinarian or zoologist or ecologist. Because the poem is long enough, I can even notice threads in her writing, like the food chain and survival: the red foxes and x-ray fish hunting and the turtle avoid-ing cars on the road. She knows that mongooses live on "scrublands," which is a word I have never heard a student use in writing before, and her closing fact about zebras was new to me too.

As a poem, this is quick and imperfect, but as a window into what this student cares about and would write about with passion, it is clear. Viewing this poem as a brainstorm for more writing, I can discuss this potential in a conference. I will bring up a few questions for Rosaleen:

> What drew you to write about nature?

> When you look over this poem, which animals here are your favor-ites? What do you love about them?

> I notice a thread of survival comes up in your poem. Tell me more about what you know about that.

> I see another thread about playfulness and joy here. What do you think we can learn about joy by watching animals?

> You could choose to write your next essay about a topic related to nature. When you look over your poem, what do you see that might make a more specific topic than nature?

> If you had to pick a line or two here that you would love to write more about (or research more about), which lines would you choose? Try writing a five-line abecedarian, A-E just about that topic.

The poem helps Rosaleen to think broadly at first but then quickly narrow these ideas down to one or two that will best point her to a topic for writing that she really cares about. Will this grow into an essay about conservation? An argument about the importance of zoos in the education of children? Will she zero in on a single food chain and examine its place in the ecosystem? She already has something down on the page. Instead of just a few options to pick from, she has twenty-six.

PRO TIP

Do your students need a bit more scaffolding to start an abecedarian poem? Try using Scaffolding Strategy 1 in Appendix A, starting an abecedarian draft as a class.

Students do not have to craft a complete abecedarian to have this effect. Even five or ten alphabetized lines help students push through some of the "I-don't-know-what-to-write-about" phase and give you something specific to discuss with a student in a conference about big ideas and concepts.

These poems do not have to be melodic or deep or meditative, though some lines might be. These poems do strip away the stigma of poetry as a stodgy, intimidating genre while also disarming our students' inner editors in the brainstorming phase, because all a rough abecedarian asks us to do is to write around a topic and build a bridge to the next letter. It is an exercise in engineering ideas.

Sometimes, as in Rosaleen's case, this becomes a type of list poem, generating a *topic* for writing. The abecedarian can also be particularly helpful in brainstorming threads of *content* to develop in a piece of writing. For a student who knows they want to write an analysis essay about a favorite movie, for example, I might say, "OK, write a quick abecedarian about your first experience ever seeing this movie. You can mention points of the plot, but don't focus on that. Include your reactions, the questions that teemed in your head while you watched it the first time, the images that made you go 'Wow!' in this movie. Once you've got that down, come back and we can talk about how these ideas might be organized into an essay on the topic."

Published abecedarians do all kinds of interesting work. In the following examples, Robert Pinsky uses the form as a meditation on mortality while Gabriel Fried creates a kind of fantastic, dreamy romp. Sam Sax and Natalie Diaz harness the power of this form as calls for action and justice, Dr. Joshua Bennett interrogates American culture, and Patricia Smith's poem responds to the trauma of Hurricane Katrina. Students may find it fascinating to eventually write this type of poem for all sorts of purposes, taking their poems through a fuller writing process and toward publication in school newspapers, literary magazines, or yearbooks.

While my students learned about this form of poetry from my mini-lesson, I learned something about its power from them. It provides the propellers young writers need at the beginning of their process *and* a structure to help them feel comfortable approaching that blank page in the notebook or face that winking cursor on the screen. Getting started becomes as easy as A-B-C.

Other Abecedarian Poems to Bring on the Brainstorms

1. "Abecedarian Requiring Further Examination of Anglikan Seraphym Subjugation of a Wild Indian Rezervation" by Natalie Diaz

2. "Abecedary" by Gabriel Fried

3. "American Abecedarian" by Dr. Joshua Bennett

4. "Antizionist Abecedarian" by Sam Sax

5. "ABC" by Robert Pinsky

6. "Siblings" by Patricia Smith

POETRY PAUSE: THE GOLDEN SHOVEL

Poem: "The Age of Information" by Brett Vogelsinger

Plan: Find an intriguing line of text. Copy the line vertically down the right side of a page, and craft a golden shovel poem based on the line.

Big Picture: Writing a "golden shovel" poem opens up a line that is already well-crafted and thought-provoking and lets a student writer expand it to show their thinking about that topic. Some of that thinking can then be used to focus a larger or longer piece in a different genre.

Scan this QR code to see the original golden shovel poem, "The Golden Shovel."

Terrence Hayes's invention of "golden shovel" poems, which follow the pattern of his original "The Golden Shovel" published in 2010, have become popular with creative writing teachers as a way for new poets to play with a published line from another text. The original by Terrence Hayes takes Gwendolyn Brooks's "We Real Cool" and concludes each line of his poem with the subsequent word from her original classic.

So in some ways, the golden shovel poem is like the abecedarian. Instead of giving a letter to start each line of the poem, it allows the writer to borrow a word to conclude each line. I like to tell students that they are engineering bridges, using one writer's words as pillars of support and stringing their own ideas, like suspension cords, between the borrowed words.

Golden shovel poems can come from lines of poetry like Terrence Hayes's original, but they do not have to. Most English teachers I know have moved to integrate more nonfiction writing and journalism into their classes in recent years. In your world, it may mean weaving more current event articles into discussions of whole-class novel studies.

I created this sample for students from the infamously misinformed headline published in the *Baltimore Evening Sun* in 1912: "All *Titanic* Passengers Are Safe; Transferred in Lifeboats at Sea." It is an early example of misinformation that made it to print. And that is the topic I explore in my poem. You will notice the original line, bold and vertically arranged on the right-hand side of the poem.

THE AGE OF INFORMATION

We want to have **all**
the information at the speed of the ***Titanic***.
We care little for the **passengers**.
We are awash in likes and sound bites and we **are**
not **safe**.

Responsibility **transferred**
to readers and viewers. The facts survive **in**
bobbing **lifeboats**.
This is where we are **at**:
Holding binoculars, we scan the tossing **sea**.

As I figured out how to get to the next word in each headline, I started thinking about how fast misinformation can spread today and imagined how the *Titanic* disaster might have sounded in the age of social media. I thought about how responsibility for information has been transferred to the consumer, and simple, pure facts feel endangered by the twenty-first-century tendency for clinging to opinion even when it directly contradicts fact. My mind wanted to keep going with these ideas after I finished writing. Thunderclouds had gathered.

After sharing my golden shovel poem, I invite students to choose a line out of an article or essay that we have read, write it one word at a time down the right-hand margin of a page in their writer's notebook, and string some ideas between those words from the author. I empha-size that the ideas should show *their* thinking on the topic, not just repeat or summarize the information they read in the article. Golden shovel poems are invitations to blend the personal with the public, our experience with our reading.

My students have also written golden shovel poems while participating in a book club unit that synchronized with their study of WWII in his-tory class. In this case, we blended poetry reading, creative writing, and reading response.

We read "First Fig," Edna St. Vincent Millay's classic poem and the source of the idiom "burning the candle at both ends," as our Poem of the Day:

FIRST FIG

by Edna St. Vincent Millay

My candle burns at both ends;
    It will not last the night;
But ah, my foes, and oh, my friends—
    It gives a lovely light!

Next, I challenge students to craft a golden shovel poem about their reading using one of the lines from this famous poem. Here is Andrew's golden shovel in which he responds to Liesel's nightmares in *The Book Thief*:

I try my hardest to not dream **it,**
I live in fear that I **will.**
But whether it plagues me or **not,**
My papa's voice will **last.**
And whenever I wake up, sweating from **the**
Memory, his tunes bring me back to only this **night.**

Gavin does the same, responding to the early scene in *Night* when Mrs. Schächter has a fevered, prophetic vision of fire:

No idea where to, **my**
people travel by the light of a **candle**
tolerating Schächter's cries of **burns**
and being grateful **at**
her quiet moments. She hallucinated **both**
times, but maybe foresaw thousands of Jews' **ends.**

After drafting these, ask your students one or more of these questions to get them thinking about further writing:

- In writing your golden shovel poem, what did you dig up and uncover?

- Now that you have drafted a golden shovel poem, what word(s) stand out most from the line in the original text?

- What is your favorite line that you wrote for this poem? What does it make you want to keep thinking about?

- How might that inform a concept for writing a longer piece?

Troy Hicks and Andy Schoenborn (2020) outline three main steps for writing teachers to take in their book *Creating Confident Writers*: invite, encourage, and celebrate. Think for a moment how writing a golden shovel poem can build a student's confidence. In drafting the poem, she has already engineered bridges between words with her own ideas. I have already *invited* her to think about an idea by borrowing another writer's lens. In a conference, I can *encourage* her to narrow her focus. While I know that very little of this golden shovel poem will make it into an essay draft, I do know that something here will be golden—true to its name—giving us something to *celebrate* in a conference. An idea is already expanding. Before the draft of a longer essay even begins, all three of these essential ingredients for writerly confidence can be built into the process of creating a golden shovel poem.

Other Golden Shovel Poems to Bring on the Brainstorm

1. "Exercise" by Irene Latham and Charles Waters from *Dictionary for a Better World* (a line from Maya Angelou)

2. "Truth" by Nikki Grimes (a line from Jean Toomer)

3. "Somebody" by Kirstine Call (a line from Emily Dickinson)

4. "Taking the High Road, Finally" by Colleen Murphy (a line from Robert Frost)

5. "The Golden Shovel" by Terrence Hayes (a line from Gwendolyn Brooks)

POETRY PAUSE: COLLECTING WORDS

Poem: "Word Collection" by Amy Ludwig VanDerwater

Plan: Students string together favorite vocabulary around a topic.

Big Picture: By collecting words before facing the pressure to write extensively in sentences and paragraphs, students gather material that will help them to have a tone of authority when they write. This also provides a bank of words students can pull from if they become tangled up in searching for the right word or articulating ideas while creating a draft.

In general, collecting words can open our eyes to new possibilities as writers. A confluence of ideas from two skilled, brilliant teachers helped me realize the brainstorming potential in word collections.

In 2018, I attended a packed presentation at NCTE in which Rebekah O'Dell shared a word-collecting strategy for writers. It was practical, simple, and profound.

She handed the audience members a brief sports analysis article to read and asked us to list words in the article that we thought were particularly well suited to any sports analysis piece, words we might even consider using to write our own sports analysis essay.

In her classroom, she later asks students to come back to that list when it's time to draft an analysis piece. If you are familiar with Rebekah O'Dell and Allison Marchetti's work, you know that this simple strategy reflects thinking from their book *Beyond Literary Analysis* (2018). A word list becomes a painter's palette of language that students can use to write about their own topic with a tone of authority.

The same year I left this presentation in awe, teacher and poet Amy Ludwig VanDerwater wrote a guest post for my annual blogging project, *Go Poems* (2018). In it, she encouraged student writers to keep a list of favorite words on a page in a notebook. Later, she advised, have them come back to that list to look for points of connection, cool sound effects, and rhythms that could string them into a poem. She modeled this with a poem of her own called "Word Collection."

A remix possibility for Rebekah and Amy's ideas struck me: Why not, after having students pull vivid, sports analysis language from a mentor text, have them write a quick, low-stakes, ten-line poem, taking the words for a test run! Sure, our final goal may be for them to use

Scan this QR code to read more about word collection poems from Amy Ludwig VanDerwater.

these words in an essay. Sure, the poem will be a little clunky, far from a masterpiece. But the poetic form pulls those powerful words they discovered closer together and quickly demonstrates how student writers can establish authority using professional, well-groomed vocabulary. Writing the poem reveals this BEFORE they go into the hours-long writing process of crafting a quality analysis essay.

Colin, one of my students and a star baseball player at our school, recently tried this after reading an analysis piece about the MLB players' contract negotiations. I told him, "As you read, find me the words that show you this writer knows the sport and knows what he is talking about." He gathered this list of baseball words that he felt contributed to the article's tone of authority.

1.1 **Ninth-grader Colin lists words from his reading that contribute to a professional tone in a sports article.**

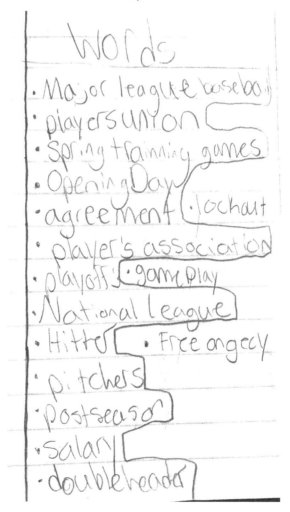

It only took about three extra minutes for him to rearrange these items into a poem. I told him, "Find what words sound cool near each other, even if they don't make perfect logical sense on the same line. Just play with these words a little bit and arrange them differently than the original list, into something that looks and sounds more like a poem. There's a poet named Christian Wiman who says 'I follow the sounds.' Another poet, Aimee Nezhukumatathil, calls it the 'snap, crackle, and pop of the language.' Try that with your arrangement of words." Here is the result of that prompt:

BASEBALL ARTICLE POEM
by Colin

Players union, players association, and spring training
Hitter vs. pitcher
Postseason playoffs
Lockout league
Agents are agreements
Doubleheader hitter up
Lockout vs. gameplay
Opening day doubleheader
Major league lockout

At this point, Colin is attending to details of the words, even the interplay of their sounds. While this is part of the art of writing a poem, the best writing in all genres has a musical lilt to it. So when it is time to write his own baseball analysis, Colin is ready to write with a word bank of rich, authoritative vocabulary *and* the more detailed knowledge of how those words sound alongside other words. He is ready to write a piece that will sound better than a draft that has not taken the time to pause for this playful preparation.

PRO TIP

Do you need to scaffold this activity a bit for your students? Create an example of your own to share with them, using Scaffolding Strategy 5 in Appendix A.

POETRY PAUSE: TILTING A TOPIC

> **Poem:** "Who Burns for the Perfection of Paper" by Martín Espada
>
> **Plan:** Students change the physical angle of their written response to a poem with a goal of aiding the fluency and diversity of their ideas around a topic.
>
> **Big Picture:** In an era where our attention span is under attack from all angles, this activity capitalizes on the power of novelty. We ask students to eschew the typical classroom expectations of straight lines and margins and let their thoughts spill over with irreverent abandon. These fluent musings provide rich springs of thought for future writing.

Not all poetry-inspired brainstorms require that students write a poem. Sometimes reading one is enough to get some raw, fresh ideas for students to explore in an analysis piece or an editorial. And literally, a new "angle" can be part of our teaching method.

For example, consider the poem "Who Burns for the Perfection of Paper" by Martín Espada.

WHO BURNS FOR THE PERFECTION OF PAPER

by Martín Espada

At sixteen, I worked after high school hours
at a printing plant
that manufactured legal pads:
Yellow paper
stacked seven feet high
and leaning
as I slipped cardboard
between the pages,
then brushed red glue
up and down the stack.
No gloves: fingertips required
for the perfection of paper,
smoothing the exact rectangle.
Sluggish by 9 PM, the hands
would slide along suddenly sharp paper,
and gather slits thinner than the crevices
of the skin, hidden.
The glue would sting,
hands oozing

till both palms burned
at the punchclock.

Ten years later, in law school,
I knew that every legal pad
was glued with the sting of hidden cuts,
that every open law book
was a pair of hands
upturned and burning.

Used with permission from Martín Espada.

For this activity, I use small photocopies of the poem to give to students. "Tape these in the middle of your writer's notebook, like you are framing it with some white space all around," I tell them.

After reading it twice, maybe discuss a question or two, such as "How has the speaker's life changed over time? How does the experience in the first stanza shape the speaker's experience in the second stanza?" Part of what I love about this poem is that it gets us thinking and talking about some extraordinary things with a topic as ordinary as paper. It asks us to weigh the hidden costs of perfection.

If your teacher mind is like mine, there is always a hum of possibility in the background as you read something new, considering how it might roll into a topic you discuss in class or a longer piece of literature you approach with your students each year. Listen to your gut. It often leads you to fresh texts that will make your classroom relevant and exciting to student writers.

This poem, for example, might introduce a longer piece of writing about power dynamics or justice or how history affects the present. An urgent, freewriting brainstorm in the white space around the poem helps students find their way to that main point. Getting their thoughts to gush helps them discover something to say and motivates them to dig deeper and write more organized commentary later.

Invite the students to turn their writer's notebook page with this poem in the middle in an unexpected way—tilt it to a 45-degree angle, turn it upside down, or lay it on its side horizontally—and write *around* the poem, fill the white space with rambling, grammatically dubious thoughts on the subject.

I tell students, "Be wild and free here! The primary goal here is to keep the pencil moving around a single thought with no editing, a true 'storm' of idea-making without any particular end goal right now."

Once again, I do not offer even a preview of the writing assignment on the horizon. In fact, if this brainstorm leads into an essay eventually, it is best to avoid mentioning that right now. Nothing kills a brainstorm faster than the prospect of a major assignment.

Here is an example from my student Susanna:

1.2 **High school student Susanna tilts a poem to explore her thinking.**

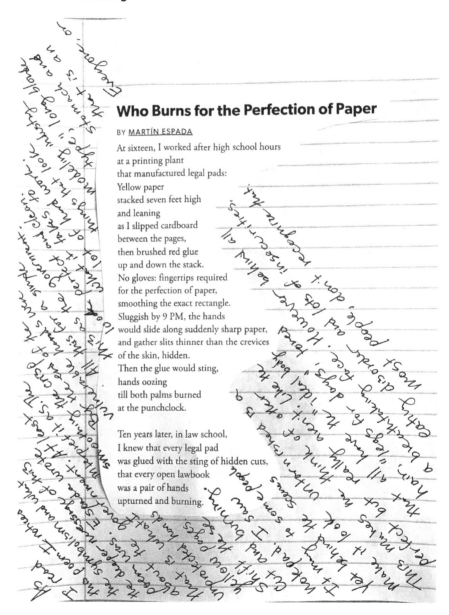

Who Burns for the Perfection of Paper

BY MARTÍN ESPADA

At sixteen, I worked after high school hours
at a printing plant
that manufactured legal pads:
Yellow paper
stacked seven feet high
and leaning
as I slipped cardboard
between the pages,
then brushed red glue
up and down the stack.
No gloves: fingertips required
for the perfection of paper,
smoothing the exact rectangle.
Sluggish by 9 PM, the hands
would slide along suddenly sharp paper,
and gather slits thinner than the crevices
of the skin, hidden.
Then the glue would sting,
hands oozing
till both palms burned
at the punchclock.

Ten years later, in law school,
I knew that every legal pad
was glued with the sting of hidden cuts,
that every open lawbook
was a pair of hands
upturned and burning.

Susanna is an experienced and confident reader. So she goes right for the gold when she tilts this poem and starts to shake out what's going on inside of it.

She first notes that there appears to be some symbolism in this poem, relates it to government, and then to the modeling industry. She writes, in part, "By the end of the shift, the vulnerable hands were cut and burning. All this for a simple notepad! . . . This makes me think of other things that look perfect but are not. Like the modeling industry. It looks beautiful . . . However behind all that is an eating disorder and lots of insecurities. Everyone, or most people, don't recognize that."

Here is how Mason responded to the same prompt:

1.3 **High school student Mason floods his page with thinking alongside the poem.**

Part of his tilted freewrite reads,

"I think it makes an interesting point as to how things we use are created. Who is making our paper? A machine? A person? A child? Who made this paper? There is obvious irony of having what can be used as a tool for change being made in horrible conditions. There is care, however, in what is being made. 'No gloves: fingertips only.' There is hidden pain in paper."

Both Susanna and Mason have quickly discovered some possible topics for writing.

My students tell me that there is something inexplicably freeing about turning a piece of paper on its head before freewriting, about seeing text at an unconventional angle as we ponder it. This kind of brainstorm is subtly subversive, like graffiti art for the notebook. It dissolves some filters that otherwise inhibit our teenaged writers from sharing their most audacious thinking.

Most of all, this helps student do the very realistic work that writers everywhere do: circling a main point like a falcon about to dive. Strangely, working in this kind of white space to brainstorm is so much less intimidating than the linear space of a traditional notebook page. Both student samples reveal possibilities for an essay have already emerged, big ideas they may find worthy of more extended exploration.

IT ALL COMES DOWN TO THIS

Writing poems at the outset of our process is disarming. In truth, teenaged writers do enjoy brainstorming, when we help them get around their own self-consciousness. Poems can help us to help them to do that. Poet William Wordsworth famously said, "Fill your paper with the breathings of your heart." I agree with him. And I might also add, "Flood your paper with stormings of your brain."

POETRY PAUSES FOR WRITING LITERARY ANALYSIS

Brainstorming celebrates the mad jumble of ideas our brains can generate and verbalize. Not everything we generate, though, is beautiful or even useful. Greg Bachman (2000), in an article about brainstorming in a corporate setting, notes that often "the brilliant ideas that bloom in brainstorming sessions wilt when taken out of the greenhouse; they're not ready for an environment so unlike the permissive, just-do-it atmosphere of the idea session" (para. 15). Part of the writing process involves identifying the best ideas, pruning and guiding them, organizing them into something that will eventually make sense to a reader.

This is particularly essential with analysis writing. If students have topics they are keen to analyze, they still sometimes struggle to know how to harness and organize these ideas into an academic essay. Literary analysis poses a particular challenge: students formulate ideas as they read, yet they cannot thoroughly analyze a book until they have finished reading it. This requires an understanding of details, a sensitivity to patterns, and a curiosity about the big-picture meaning after they have finished a book. How can poetry pauses help our students to write excellent analysis of the literature they read?

Rather than a barrage of ideas like the last chapter, this chapter begins with two quick poetry pauses that scratch the surface of theme and character analysis. Then, we will dive deeper with two poetry pauses that assist students in prewriting an essay about a literary theme, a required summative assessment in the course I teach. My hope is that you might lay this central example from my school's curriculum like an old-school transparency film over a major assignment in *your* curriculum and find that these poetry pauses help your students organize their analytical thinking around the literature you study together.

POETRY PAUSE: FRAMES FOR ANALYSIS

Poem: "Jurassic World" by Brett Vogelsinger

Plan: A simple poetry frame helps students tease out the many possibilities for analysis in a text or story.

Big Picture: It's hard to think about complexity. In a world where attention spans feel ever-shortened by technology, anxiety, and disruption fatigue, it is too easy to oversimplify our thinking and never nurture truly interesting analysis. This frame reminds us that all sorts of stories have complexity and room to explore with analysis.

Sometimes the best way to coax our students into writing literary analysis is to demonstrate how full of possibility analytical writing can be. This might mean beginning with movie, music, sports, TV series, or political analysis. If we can help students to write about parts of a whole, to see how the bits of something affect the big picture on a topic that they already find engaging, it's a big win!

We can pause and give students a fill-in-the-blank poetic frame. This creates a Mad-Lib experience for students that feels manageable and welcoming.

One frame I created to start thinking about analysis looks like this:

(Insert title of work being analyzed) is not just about _____.

It's about _____,

_____,

_____.

It's about _____ and

_____.

It's about _____

and _____ and _____ .

Here's a sample poem about a movie that I created using this frame:

> *Jurassic World* is not just about dinosaurs.
> It's about capitalism,
> man's desire to create,
> our thirst for spectacle.
> It's about Chris Pratt's performance
> and CGI artwork.
> It's about science
> and family and in-the-moment problem solving.

After a quickwrite draft of this list poem, students might reorganize their ideas into a pattern that will work for a draft. For my *Jurassic World* example, I invite them to work with me on sorting out what I discovered: "Let's prioritize here. To analyze what makes *Jurassic World* tick, which of these is most important to talk about first? Which ideas are a lot alike and might be combined into one paragraph in an analysis article?"

We reorganize the poem together on the projector screen. As a class, we notice that some of what I listed has to do with performance, some with design, and some with themes. In so doing, we have created a skeleton for an entire film analysis.

Students can then apply this strategy to the work they have chosen to analyze: a new bill proposed in Congress, a local news story, a painting, an album . . . the list goes on and on.

PRO TIP

If you need to streamline this activity, use the first reproducible handout in Appendix B to put this frame at your students' fingertips.

This is only one frame, of course, that hinges on the word *about*. Try creating similar frames tailored to your particular assignments. Craft a sample to share with your students to show them how the frame can be helpful. The frames create a low-pressure writing challenge that breaks the ice and gets some preliminary analysis down on the page.

POETRY PAUSE: ANALYZING CHARACTER AND CONFLICT

Poem: "Sisters" by Janet Wong

Plan: We hollow out an existing poem to rewrite it with content from our independent reading books with an aim to analyze character and conflict.

Big Picture: Even in books that they thoroughly comprehend, students sometimes struggle to put into words the nature of tensions and conflicts between characters that are not directly stated and explained in the novel. A poem that captures some of this in just six lines with a little figurative language helps students to articulate some starter ideas for character analysis.

Janet Wong's poem "Sisters" is wonderful for several reasons: it is at once straightforward, figurative, and universal. This makes it a perfect Poem of the Day for a quick analysis of character and conflict in my students' independent reading books.

Before we read this poem, I make sure students know the words *tofu* and *ginger* since the figurative language of the poem depends upon these two words. A quick slide with two photos helps most students realize they have some familiarity with the two foods, their textures and flavors.

SISTERS

by Janet Wong

She calls me tofu
because I am so soft,
easily falling apart.

I wish I were tough
and full of fire, like ginger —
like her.

From *A Suitcase of Seaweed & More*, 1996, 2019.

First, I ask, "How does the speaker in the poem feel about her sister?" I love the spectrum of responses this question provokes, everything from "admiration" to "overshadowed by her sister" to "jealous." And for a short poem, there is a lot going on! Ultimately, there is tension between two people, and similar tension is at the core of any novel students read. The best novels have characters with complex, intriguing tensions between them, though students are not always adept at interpreting them and putting these tensions into the language of literary analysis.

Together, we hollow out the poem on the whiteboard, taking out the parts that make the poem unique to this speaker and leaving in the tendons, the connective language that holds the poem's intriguing tension. Then I say, "Try making this a poem about a character in the book you are reading."

Hannah writes about a character in her book:

> He calls me insensitive
> because I am so harsh,
> saying vulgar words like rapid fire.
>
> I wish I were sweet
> and loving, like a warm blanket –
> like him.

And Billy's rendition, for a different book, sounds like this:

> She calls me weak
> because I am crying,
> easily upset.
>
> I wish I were stronger
> and braver, like rock –
> like my wife.

PRO TIP

This poem also has a handout ("Character and Conflict") in Appendix B and on the companion website if you need to streamline this activity.

You might notice that my students have not transferred figurative language as tidily as I imagined they would. Neither of these examples emulated the metaphor in the opening line of the original poem.

What they *did* accomplish was giving words to an ongoing conflict between characters in a book. They assumed the point of view of one of the characters for six lines and thought about how that character might regard another person in the book. They found some words that might be the seeds of a topic sentence or thesis statement for a bit of character analysis. And they did it in six lines.

As an alternate plan, I could ask students to approach analysis by thinking about the setting and what it would have to say about the plot of a novel. When studying *Lord of the Flies*, Aum wrote this poem from the island's point of view and even embedded two vocabulary words from the unit!

They left a scar on my chin.
It didn't hurt, but I still felt it.
They plucked at my beard for fruit.
They ripped my pliant hair to use it as shelter.
I let it be . . . until they climbed on my nose
and lit it. It burned like alcohol
on a cut. What annoyed me the most
was their ludicrous behavior.

Whether using a poetry frame or a simple prompt like the one just above, when we finish, the class has some good raw materials to work with.

PRO TIP

The question "What is your best discovery here?" helps student writers to reflect on their thinking during a poetry pause.

"Circle what you want to bring from this poem into some analysis writing," I tell them. "If it's a line, a word, or the whole poem's big idea, all of that works. What is your best discovery here?"

Asking students this question empowers them to feel that *they* are doing the work of analysis right from the start. I am not handing them a main point they must develop. I am not sharing my point of view on the book or characters. They uncover something worth wrestling with a bit and writing about, and that is the thrill of genuine analysis in the first place. It is why the genre exists.

THE LITERARY THEME ESSAY

Where I teach, all high school freshmen are required to write an essay that identifies and analyzes the central theme in a novel. This is not a revolutionary assignment, and somewhere along the line in middle and high school I am sure it is an assignment every student receives, possibly more than once.

By the time we reach this point in the year, my students have some experience writing analysis outside of literature and our class discussions of reading. Articulating a theme that they feel is worthy of their extended attention and study is still a challenge.

Additionally, we write this essay after a period of independent reading, so students are examining themes from an array of books that I may not know as well as some of the core curriculum texts that we read as a class. This makes reading their essays enjoyable but helping them organize and focus their ideas difficult.

Pausing to craft poetry is one way to make writing literary analysis of a novel more approachable. It helps students dig deeper into details they later incorporate into the heart of their writing. Prewriting with poetry can give literary analysis essays a pulse.

PAUSING TO PREWRITE AS WE READ

I learned that this eye-catching color wheel is called "Plutchik's wheel of emotions" from the YA author Amy Sarig King, who shared it during a conference presentation (Adams et al., 2019). Its creator, psychologist Robert Plutchik, aimed to help people identify and clarify their emotions by organizing and categorizing them, even labeling the white space between each color to show where emotions mix and merge. For example, joy and anticipation together create optimism. Opposite emotions are opposite each other on the wheel.

2.1 Plutchik's Wheel of Emotions

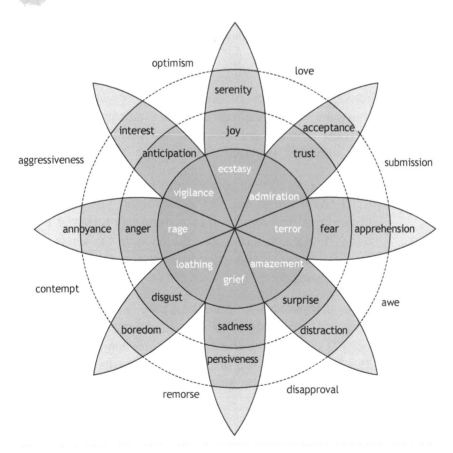

Public domain.

While the wheel is excellent for naming and sorting our own emotions, I realized how valuable this visual aid could be for talking about characters and noticing the changes they experience, emotionally, across the arc of a novel.

Returning from this conference presentation to my students and their independent reading books, I changed my traditional approach to our theme essay. Instead of haunting them with reminders of an impending "major theme essay assignment" the whole time they read their novels, I gave them this challenge:

> Pick two characters to follow through the book. Four times during the plot, pinpoint the emotional state of each of these characters on this wheel. Explain in a quick annotation what circumstances have led each character to experience the emotion.

I am in a building with a 1-to-1 Microsoft program, so my students logged these brief observations on a personal OneNote page. In a lower-tech setting, I would have given each student a photocopied image of the Plutchik's wheel to color and tape in their writer's notebook to record these observations in the surrounding white space.

But let's get back to the good stuff . . . the writing.

After students logged their observations on Plutchik's wheel, I asked them to write a poem in four stanzas, capturing the changes in one of the characters they followed and providing slightly more context for that character's emotional journey.

PRO TIP

Scaffolding Strategy 5 in Appendix A works well here if you need it. I share an example from my own notebook with "Romeo" at the top of the page with "sadness/ecstasy/rage/grief" spaced out evenly down the rest of the page, ready for writing.

"Take a blank page in your writer's notebook," I say, "and write the name of one of the characters you have been observing at the top. Then take those four different emotions you noticed throughout the book, in the same order you noticed them, and space them out over the rest of the page, leaving some blank lines between each emotion."

"Now that we have a frame, let's take each of these emotions and turn it into a short stanza of a poem. Let yourself write it like you are *this* character, feeling *this* emotion. This is not a summary, just a raw look at what the character goes through with a few short words for each of these emotions."

Each point my students labeled on their copy of Plutchik's wheel while reading becomes its own stanza in the poem.

Ava R. read *All the Bright Places* by Jennifer Niven and followed Finch and Violet's emotions through the story. Figure 2.2 shows her Plutchik wheel:

2.2 Ava R.'s Plutchik Wheel for *All the Bright Places* by Jennifer Niven

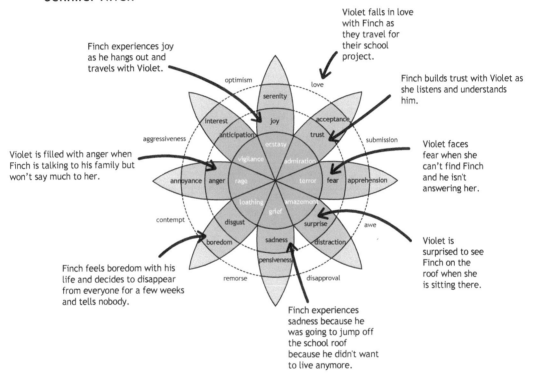

Finch experiences joy as he hangs out and travels with Violet.

Violet falls in love with Finch as they travel for their school project.

Finch builds trust with Violet as she listens and understands him.

Violet is filled with anger when Finch is talking to his family but won't say much to her.

Violet faces fear when she can't find Finch and he isn't answering her.

Finch feels boredom with his life and decides to disappear from everyone for a few weeks and tells nobody.

Violet is surprised to see Finch on the roof when she is sitting there.

Finch experiences sadness because he was going to jump off the school roof because he didn't want to live anymore.

She chose to base her four-stanza poem on her observations about Finch, shown in Figure 2.3. (Spoiler alert: If this book is on your TBR list, only read the first two stanzas!)

2.3 Ava R.'s Four-Stanza Poem in Response to *All the Bright Places* by Jennifer Niven

finch ③
Traveling sends electricity through your blood
Joy — Seeing the World
and discovering it's joys
Seeing sights you will never forget

Trust — Being with someone, not alone
telling them everything
and pouring out your soul
builds a stronger than life connection

boredom

Sitting, watching, listening
the clock pauses still
nothing moves, nothing happens
a daze falls upon us

Sadness — feeling empty and alone
with no one but yourself
tears fill eyes
as sadness overcomes you
Brain dead
drained from everything
The endless amount of work
the few calming hours of sleep

Michael chose to follow Josef and Isabel through *Refugee* by Alan Gratz. While reading, he created the Plutchik wheel shown in Figure 2.4, then wrote the poem to trace Isabel's emotional journey:

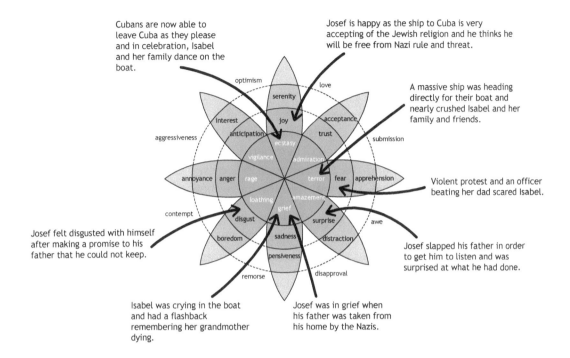

Cubans are now able to leave Cuba as they please and in celebration, Isabel and her family dance on the boat.

Josef is happy as the ship to Cuba is very accepting of the Jewish religion and he thinks he will be free from Nazi rule and threat.

A massive ship was heading directly for their boat and nearly crushed Isabel and her family and friends.

Violent protest and an officer beating her dad scared Isabel.

Josef felt disgusted with himself after making a promise to his father that he could not keep.

Josef slapped his father in order to get him to listen and was surprised at what he had done.

Isabel was crying in the boat and had a flashback remembering her grandmother dying.

Josef was in grief when his father was taken from his home by the Nazis.

Fear
Her father, her protector, her hero:
beaten,
cowering.

Ecstasy.
Escape, freedom, safety,
the protests left behind.

Terror.
Waves part, rolling out a red carpet for:
a ship, a killer.

Grief.
Death, the photographer of her memories:
Her grandfather's hand reaching out of the water.

You probably notice that these short, quick poems provide valuable reflections about a character in a novel. But how might these observations enhance a student's essay about theme?

Teachers know that themes are not clinical, some kind of chip inserted just beneath the skin of the story by the author. They are organic, like vessels and capillaries; they weave in and out of every muscle and joint of the novel. Themes pulse through the main characters, people who—if the author succeeds—feel as real as our friends or foes, who bring us to laughter and tears alongside them.

So by tracing a character's emotions, struggles, and changes, we can also infer the themes in the book and the way these big ideas impact individual humans. This helps students elaborate when it is time to write about the book. They revisit and reflect on the major turning points and the critical decisions of the characters, some of the moments where themes become most apparent in novels.

Consider Owen B. and his work on the main character, Jay, from Randy Ribay's *Patron Saints of Nothing*. On his wheel, Owen notes Jay's emotional movement through remorse, interest, disapproval, and trust.

In one stanza he looks at Jay's interest in his cousin's death:

> But the interest of
> why they left you
> rises above everything
> and you need to figure out why.

This thinking eventually found its way into his essay draft in this snippet of analysis:

> When a loved one dies, no one can focus, no one has a care about anything else, and there is no exception to how Jay is feeling. Being a senior in high school puts a lot of pressure on teenagers, the workload, the grades, thinking about college, but at this point, the only thing Jay can think about is his dead cousin. Jay's head is stuck in thought only about Jun. He says, "Besides, Jun's death has me looking at things differently. Like, if I complete my assignments or not, what does it really matter?" (Ribay, p. 29). Everyone has thought about something like this at least once, maybe even many times, all they care about is the passing of their loved one, and they do not care about school or anything else like that because they are so stuck in their sorrow.

Later in his poem, registering the emotion "disapproval," he writes,

> Once finding out,
> the disapproval is the
> only thing you're worried about.
> You disapproved of the way he died,
> you disapprove of how
> he died, you disapprove
> of why he died.

This thinking found its way from his quick poem into part of the conclusion of his theme essay:

> In *Patron Saints of Nothing*, there is so much family aspect. The whole plot is about family and the realization of what is going on in the world. Jay, after plenty of time playing video games, finally ventures out into the real world as he finds out that his cousin Jun has passed. He makes the realization that family is everything, and to him, that is way more important than anything else. *Patron Saints of Nothing* has an aspect of non-fiction to it; the plot is fiction, but the whole drug war, President Duterte, it is all real.

In *Patron Saints of Nothing*, Jay's disapproval of his family's reaction to Jun's death is complicated by his new understanding of the drug war and how it affects individuals and families in the Philippines, and Owen's draft reveals that he understands this important element of his character. This gives him more interesting, specific things to say about the theme he explores in this essay.

In short, pausing to name the character's emotions throughout the book and write a poem about them adds depth to students' literary analysis. Writing this poem slows down their contemplation before a rough draft, infuses heart and voice into their observations, and gives them both time and words to flesh out their ideas more deeply in a literary analysis essay.

The process is also a good return on investment because it steals time from neither the reading nor the drafting process. The brief notes students take while reading are quick and pre-organized, even color-coded. Plutchik's wheel urges students to think in a way that prepares them for their upcoming writing without hounding them with pesky "major assignment" reminders. The poems they draft become quick prewrites for a longer piece, yet they also sometimes stand alone as quality creative writing.

And even students whose poems were not a resounding success have taken time to give words to emotions, a worthy, mindful endeavor that supports social emotional health in our students. As Carol Jago says, "Let's teach SEL through literature." I'm sure she would not mind me adding "and through writing about it."

STATING A THEME

Once we have compiled observations from our reading, and we begin to tease out the themes from a book, my students tend to face a few challenges:

- Students want to write out the theme as a single word: friendship, war, revenge. They have heard from past teachers that themes are more complex than this, but they have trouble retaining and/or applying that knowledge from year to year.

- Students who do craft sentence-length themes, sometimes settle too quickly on greeting card clichés ("The author develops the theme 'You can't judge a book by its cover'") or a rather sterile tone ("The author develops the theme 'It takes a lot of determination to overcome obstacles'").

- Students sometimes struggle with the inference skills to pull broader ideas from a plot in an independent reading book. We work with this during reading conferences, but by the end of the book, some have a hard time cinching their observations succinctly in a statement of theme.

Near the end of their independent reading books, but before I explain the theme assignment, I invite students to craft one more tiny poem in their writer's notebooks. I want to lead them into a well-worded statement of a theme from their recent reading.

We all begin the draft of our poems with the same first line: "My author has something to say," replacing "my author" with the author's full name. I write my version, based on the book I am currently reading, under the document camera as my students write. Here are a few results from my students' notebooks:

Ava wrote about the *Mulan* novel by Grace Lin, while Christian applied the poetic format to his understanding of *Walden*.

Mulan

Grace Lin has something
to say:

Following your own expectations
can grant you satisfaction
from the world.
Even if the world expects
more or different.

Walden

Henry David Thoreau
has something
to say:

Don't get caught up
in material things.
Don't turn your wants
into needs.

A simple way of life
is a better way of life.

A model citizen
should govern himself.
Less government
is better government.

The pattern works well for all sorts of genres including Ryan's work
with Phil Knight's business memoir, *Shoe Dog*.

Shoe Dog

Phil Knight has
something
to say:

Not everything will go to plan.
The unexpected always arrives
but take the risk and
you can accomplish great
things.

And some students used their poetic license to be slightly more verbose and develop their ideas with a bit more figurative perspective, as Luke did in his work with the Matthew Landis novel *It's the End of the World As I Know It*.

2.5 Luke's Poem About Matthew Landis's Novel *It's the End of the World As I Know It*

Matthew Landis
has something
to say!

Planning for something that
wasn't planned

These plans may never end
with "wer" and begin with "ans"

This life will throw
a curveball in a full count

Starting at your head
landing at your laces

leaving you dumbstruck
Relying on empty faces

But you have to get up
Just like Rocky said

And push forward so you
can hopefully see the promised land

This activity requires less than five minutes and addresses all three of the major concerns I have seen with this essay assignment in the past.

- Students naturally identify, or at least approach, one of the major themes in the book and do so with more than a single word.

- Student word choice tends to be more vivid, less cliché, because I have asked them to craft their idea as a poem. Our daily exposure to quality poems at the start of class helps with this, but teachers who have woven even *some* poetry into their lessons and writer's notebook work during the term will find that almost every student succeeds in this initial poem-crafting. This is especially true when I create an example in real time alongside my students.

- Providing students with a sentence frame makes the inferential nature of theme less intimidating. Authors have observations to share, things to say to the world. The frame invites each student to take two minutes and tease out one of these ideas.

This is elemental prewriting for an essay about a theme in a text. It is also a poem. Poetry becomes prewriting, a tiny but impactful part of the process for writing a longer literary analysis essay.

IT ALL COMES DOWN TO THIS

The limited space and tight structure of a poem can give students a trellis to climb with their ideas, a way to begin their analytical thinking in words that are crisp and clear. No matter the genre, those two ideals matter.

For a teacher who has never used poetry in the way this chapter describes, these methods may sound convoluted and time-consuming at first. I promise you, they are not. The more we embed quickwrite poetry into our students' notebook routine, the more it becomes part of their thinking routine, and the more fluent their writing becomes. It does not take long for this to happen, and soon poetry pauses like these are welcome respites from the more arduous parts of English class, and yet . . . shhh, don't tell them . . . they warm us up for the heavy lifting later in the writing process.

3

POETRY PAUSES FOR CRAFTING NARRATIVE

THE INFLUENCE OF POETRY ON TWENTY-FIRST-CENTURY NARRATIVE WRITERS

There has been a growing crossover during the past twenty years between the genres of poetry and narrative writing. For many teachers and students, their first introduction to the novel-in-verse may have been, appropriately enough, Kwame Alexander's 2014 book *The Crossover*. This book had a winning combination of relatable plot and characters told in swift and agile verse with a cover that drew in the star athletes in the class and transformed them into star readers of poetry.

Novels-in-verse are not the only way poetry has been influencing twenty-first-century narrative writing, so when I assert that poetry writing can help students improve their own narratives, I invoke LeVar Burton's immortal words from *Reading Rainbow*: "But you don't have to take my word for it!" Consider these examples:

- Gae Polisner's September 11 novel, *The Memory of Things*, integrates two points of view, one of them in verse that gradually shifts toward traditional prose by the end of the book.

- Delia Owens (*Where the Crawdads Sing*) and Jeff Zentner (*In the Wild Light*) have written traditional novels with characters who are poets; they have crafted and embedded original poems in the voices of their characters.

- Some of your students can sing the hip-hop poetry of Lin-Manuel Miranda's biographical *Hamilton* on demand, reciting bits of history as they do so.

- Margarita Engle has published a complete Hispanic history of America in chronological history-in-verse with her book *Dreams From Many Rivers*.

- Juan Felipe Herrera has woven autobiography, picture book, and poem all into his book *Imagine*.

- In the novel-in-verse *Rez Dogs*, Joseph Bruchac explores the historical effects of epidemics on Native American communities through the lens of a contemporary teen visiting her grandparents on a reservation at the start of the COVID-19 pandemic.

- Two influential writers for young people published their memoirs in verse in recent years: Nikki Grimes (*Ordinary Hazards*) and Laurie Halse Anderson (*Shout*).

Why do the experts, the published writers our students know so well, feel that writing poetry is important? How has it influenced their story telling and their craft?

Our students may be interested to know that many novelists have been unpublished poets for years.

Jason Reynolds has been writing poetry since he was a teenager, and first discovered the power of words when sharing one of his poems at a relative's funeral (Reynolds, 2018). Only years later, after publishing more traditional narrative writing, did he publish the magnificent *Long Way Down* and *For Every One*.

Laurie Halse Anderson also started writing poetry in high school, but only after twenty years of publishing traditional narrative did she return to it for *Shout*. Why? In an interview with *Salon* she states, "When you're putting together a narrative that's in prose, there are a lot of words that don't come with hammers attached. But in a poem, you've a lot of hammers and also, in between poems in a book, there's a space for the reader to breathe and to sit with what they've just experienced in the poem" (as cited in Williams, 2019, para. 16). Nikki Grimes goes so far as to describe poetry as her "second language" and says, "I don't know that I could have written *Ordinary Hazards* any other way" (as cited in Cheaney, 2020, para. 13).

In an interview about *Where the Crawdads Sing*, a journalist asked Delia Owens about her own "relationship with poetry." Owens responded,

> I've written poetry all my life. I'm not saying I'm good at it at all. Words just come to my mind a lot. I feel a lot when I write poetry. I feel that the words themselves can be so inspiring to readers. Most people who love good prose and literature, even if they don't have time or the inclination to read poetry, when they do read a verse, they feel a lot. That was the number one thing I wanted about this book. I wanted people to feel. (Cited in Z. Owens, 2019, 16:30)

In Owens's comments, I notice this detail: Even people who do not have to or want to develop the skills of a published poet can still write poetry that comes from a place of joy. They can find joy in thinking poetically and shaping things into poetic language. This symbiotically supports their storytelling skills, even if the writer never publishes poems in literary magazines. All students can apply the lessons of poetry to their own narrative writing. To borrow Laurie Halse Anderson's metaphor, we can equip them with hammers.

POETRY PAUSES DURING NARRATIVE DRAFTS

Over time, I have learned that poetry pauses fit into different stages of the writing process depending on the genre. In our analysis chapter, the poetry pauses predominated during prewriting. They help writers organize and direct their ideas. Narrative writing is different.

PRO TIP

If you want to use poetry pauses in prewriting a narrative, consider adapting the Plutchik's wheel example from the last chapter. Invite students to map out the progression of the main character's emotions in *their* story, crafting a poem based on this before moving into more traditional storytelling.

Once students have a narrative in mind to write—whether fictional or personal—they tend to get down to the business of drafting it, to "telling their story." That does not mean the first draft is very good, but the basic idea of a narrative arc, a story having a beginning, middle, and end, is so engrained from elementary school that secondary students do not tend to struggle getting started, at least once they have gotten past the chronic "nothing exciting has ever happened to me" complaint about the personal narrative.

Most organically, poetry writing offers us some of the best possibilities during revision of our narratives. While students may know how to tell a story, they usually struggle knowing when to slow down and show us the pollen on the legs of the bumble bee in the garden, when to explode the climactic moment into a slow-motion spectacle, how to move a personal anecdote from something that merely entertains to something that engrosses and enlightens.

Will Storr says, in his book *The Science of Storytelling* (2020), that "the challenge that any of us faces is grabbing and keeping the attention of other people's brains," and that "storytellers engage a number of neural processes . . . waiting to be played like instruments in an orchestra: moral outrage, unexpected change, status play, specificity, curiosity, and so on" (p. 6). Poets are experts at these orchestrations. Narrative writers can learn a lot from them when it is time to revise and heighten the impact of their story.

POETRY PAUSE: ZOOMING IN ON KEY DETAILS

> **Poems:** "The Harvest" by Karen Blomain and "Poem Written in the Parking Lot of a Tattoo Shop While Waiting for an Appointment" by Ariel Francisco
>
> **Plan:** Students notice how poets zoom in on key details that bring the writing to life and apply zooming techniques to their revision.
>
> **Big Picture:** Sometimes in their rough drafts of narratives, students use imagery that appeals to only one of the five senses or images that are broad and vague. Poems can help them to find where more nitty-gritty details are needed in their work and find the words to develop them.

When speaking with students, I make a big deal of out of the fact that the word *revision* is the prefix *re-* followed by the root word *vision*; it contains the idea of "seeing again," approaching our work with fresh eyes. Often this involves thinking through the level of detail we develop and whether we are doing a good job of helping the reader feel like they inhabit the story or at least that they are watching it on the big screen in surround sound.

One poem that author John Green remembers from his high school years is Marianne Moore's "Poetry." He says, "There's a line in it about 'imaginary gardens with real toads in them,' and for me that's what fiction writing is" (Green, 2019, 0:19). Reading poetry helps our students to bring those toads to life, honing the detail and dimensions of their imagery. Poets and narrative writers aim to capture the imagery in a scene that best sets the mood, develops the character, or simply makes the whole piece feel more "real."

Many poems make excellent mentors for this skill and only require a few minutes to read twice.

The poem "The Harvest" by Karen Blomain is one excellent mentor text. In this poem, the speaker remembers canning the harvest with her grandmother.

THE HARVEST

by Karen Blomain

In August we can, last chore
before school. Fruit and vegetables
chosen curbside at dawn from the huckster's
truck or picked fresh from the kitchen patch
to chop, peel, stir, skim the dross, cook
down. Nanna lays on the orange rubber collar,
taps once to seal. The jars clatter and clang
like dancers in a wild boil atop the stove.
Behind the thick door, a dirt floor, the cold
air a muzzle. Silent in the spidery light
of a hung bulb, we work. Amid ancient webs,
rows of mason jars gleam in a rainbow of peaches
and pears, sweet cherries like clotted eyes
bobbing in their liquor. Above, all manner
of green—leaf and bean—chunked, cubed,
sliced and pickled. Chow-chow confettied
red and piccalilli—summer light
for a February table. We do it right:
clear the webs, line the shelves with brown
paper, then wash last year's jars.
The walls weep for our efforts.
Sometimes fragments of voices, miners
working inside the shaft just feet
away, float toward us on the moist air,
the scrape of tool and long grunt
at the heft. Burrowed in the glisten
of anthracite, they struggle with elements
older than language. Nanna starts
the tune she comforts with, *Tura-lura-lura,*
Tura-lura-lie and behind the wall a true
tenor holds the last note sure as any canary.
At the whistle, down from the breaker
they come, blinking at clouds
veined with peach-tinted light. Arms and torsos

stiff with dried silt, they nod to us on the porch
cleaning tomorrow's batch. We count the cars,
each a small hill of coal, as the 4:15
drags out of town, our hands snapping,
our aprons filled with the last summer green.

"The Harvest" by Karen Blomain, *Karen Blomain: Greatest Hits 1980-2005*, Pudding House Publications, 2005.

The poem is full of beautiful visual imagery, filled with color and light. But it also has tactile imagery in its list of verbs like "chop, peel, stir, skim the dross," "chunked, cubed,/ sliced," and sound imagery too: that "clatter and clang" of the jars that dance in boiling water, and the lyrics of her Nanna's calming song, answered in tenor from the mineshaft that runs alongside the root cellar's walls.

I ask students, "Where do you see the poet zoom in on detailed images you can picture in your mind?" and then follow up with, "What about the other five senses? The word *imagery* relates to the verb *imagine*, so where does the poet help us *imagine* something that's not visual, something we can hear or taste or touch?" Food poems are always particularly good for exploring imagery because the mere mention of food nudges readers toward taste and smell, color and texture and temperature, engaging many of the five senses. You might enjoy exploring five other food poems, listed in the box.

Five Favorite Food Poems

1. "Everybody Made Soups" by Lisa Coffman
2. "Pot Roast" by Mark Strand
3. "From Blossoms" by Li-Young Lee
4. "Nine Spice Mix" by Zeina Azzam
5. "Blackberry-Picking" by Seamus Heaney

Scan this QR code to explore five other food poems that engage the five senses well.

In a poem like "The Harvest," it is also worth pointing out that the wall between male and female domains in an old mining town is part of how the imagery operates. There are "arms and torsos/stiff with dried silt" next to the "aprons filled with the last summer green." As the poet herself says, "The seasonal women's work is juxtaposed against the work of the men in the mines, labor that was the same all year long" (Blomain, 2005, p. 4).

The poet is not zooming in on random things here. She is examining a contrast between what changes and what is constant, between labor in light and labor in darkness, between the "rainbow of peaches" on the shelf and the "clouds/veined with peach-tinted light" that the miners only get to see in the summer with its longer days. She is not in a rush. She wants you, the reader, to live this experience alongside her, as all good storytellers do.

It impresses me how many students have generational food stories to share, and it's not a bad prompt to have students quickly draft a poem in their notebooks that revolves around food and employs three of the five senses. Even a verse about microwaving a Hot Pocket can achieve that goal.

A poem that works similarly to Blomain's poem but in a more contemporary setting is this poem by Ariel Francisco:

POEM WRITTEN IN THE PARKING LOT OF A TATTOO SHOP WHILE WAITING FOR AN APPOINTMENT

by Ariel Francisco

Sun sets like a man leaving his day job
to get to his night job on time. Oh, me?
I'm in search of any kind of permanence,
sitting in my car, watching the unreliable
light bleed out on the horizon, listening
to the minutes drift like smoke into nothing.
Nothing stays in this world— it is known—
yet I too will bleed in foolish defiance.

"Poem Written in the Parking Lot of a Tattoo Shop While Waiting for An Appointment" by Ariel Francisco. *Tinderbox Poetry Journal*, Volume 4, Issue 4.

The title introduces the image of a tattoo, and fresh blood makes an appearance twice in this poem, first as a figurative image and then as literal bleeding. But we also have the sunset, a man leaving his day job, liquified light, and drifting smoke.

After reading this poem, challenge students to return to their narrative draft. I challenge them by saying this: "Enter the mind of one the main characters. Have that character pause and stare off at something on the horizon. It could be sky itself, like in Francisco's poem, but it could also be a far-off tree, a water tower, a soaring bird, or the silhouette of an approaching character. In that pause, write a poem in the character's voice. What are they thinking about, wondering, or wanting? What similes might leak into their thinking, the same way the man leaving work and the smoke leaks into Francisco's piece?"

We might even alter the first two lines of the poem if a student is stuck and says, "I can't think of anything." Your character is staring at the sunset and writes:

The sun sets like a _____

to _____. Oh me?

I'm _____

Where would this character take the poem from there?

After pausing for poetry that zoomed in on detailed imagery, Anthony crafted these sentences in his personal narrative:

> Appreciating the scenery, such as the other trees, small canopies created by hollow bushes and the winding creek, I slowly trekked my way back home, back through the walkway, over the creek and through the thorns, when my house came back in sight. . . . [I] slept like a baby that night, my thoughts filled with peace, calm, and trees.

Liam brought similar zooming techniques to his fictional horror story where a character smashes a picture frame:

> When the frame hit the wall, the photo was released from its glass and wood prison and descended slowly to the ground, like a freed bird savoring its first glide after being released from a cage. The small circles under his arms had grown even larger and Howard, who was now trembling all over, rose from his chair to clean up the wreckage. Trembling with fear, his heart beating fast enough to worry any doctor, he moved the anvils on the end of his legs where his feet should have been, one in front of the other, growing ever closer to the sight of the mess.

These five minutes spent in the writer's notebook may provide students with a new image or passage to include in the narrative. But even if it does not accomplish this word-for-word transfer, it will take the student writer deeper into the mind of their character. That is time well spent during revision. And if it is a personal narrative and the main character is your student, it provides the pause for reflection that will take their narrative beyond the "here's-what-happened-when" sort of fare and into the "here's-why-it-mattered" kind of thought we hope to uncover in a memoir.

POETRY PAUSE: ESTABLISHING IMAGES TO ANCHOR A NARRATIVE

Poem: "Wooden Church" by Charles Simic

Plan: Students sketch four quick images that will anchor their narrative writing.

Big Picture: This activity helps students to use imagery to think about their audience. What are the key images the *reader* should take away from their writing? What would they want a *reader* to be able to sketch clearly after reading their narrative?

Filmmakers use storyboards to visualize a movie before it exists. Students can practice a simplified version of this to help them anchor their storytelling in imagery as they draft their own narrative.

Scan this QR code to read "Wooden Church" by Charles Simic.

In their writer's notebooks, I ask my students to create two foursquare (sometimes called windowpane) organizers on the same page. To fill in the first one, we read a poem, "Wooden Church" by Charles Simic. You can scan the QR code to read the entire poem.

The poem describes an abandoned church, but really any poem that is evocative of a location and stimulates the five senses with its language can work for this. We take three minutes after reading the poem aloud to sketch out four images that stand out most to us as readers at the end of the poem. Notice Aum's example in Figure 3.1.

After this, we move to the second windowpane organizer. This time I say, "Think of the personal narrative we are working on right now. What are the four images you want your readers to be able to sketch out when they are done reading your piece? What do you hope they will imagine most clearly?"

We take three more minutes and give this a try, followed by a turn-and-talk to share the images they plan to include in their writing. As always, talking through a narrative during the writing process has benefits for the writer. This pause pulls the writer's attention away from plot and character for a moment to imagine the sensory details.

3.1 Student sketches in a windowpane organizer based on key images from a poem.

Figure 3.2 shows sample sketches from Aum's own narrative about arriving home as a family and realizing there had been a burglary while they were out:

3.2 Student sketches in a windowpane organizer based on key images from a personal experience.

PRO TIP

Need to draw attention to imagery later in the revision process? Scan this QR code for a web-exclusive poetry pause on the companion website using C. D. Wright's poem "The Flame."

Without a vast investment of time, Aum has visualized key images for his narrative, and this organizer anchors the rest of the drafting process. When it is time to confer or to revise, this little bit of sketching helps students empathize with their readers.

During revision I can say, "Look at your work and decide: Are these images present and powerful in this piece?" Or for peer review, we can encourage, "After your conference, ask your partner, Do these four images stand out? Is there one that needs to be a bit brighter in the draft?"

This little bridge between reading a poem that captures a vivid setting and writing a life story that produces the same results in writing that is lively and easy to imagine keeps the audience at the forefront of craft decisions.

POETRY PAUSE: MAKING MOVEMENT HAPPEN

Poems: "The Shell" by Jeff Zentner and "Big Snow" by Philip Gross

Plan: Students talk about the "rhetorical momentum" of a poem and look for ways to apply this type of movement to their narrative writing.

Big Picture: By noticing how a poem takes its readers from "Point A" to "Point B," students are better prepared to embed a meaningful arc into their personal narratives. Thinking of the audience, they consider the "so what?" of the story, step back, and elaborate on its meaning.

Poets illuminating the extraordinary in something ordinary was not new to me when I first started reading Billy Collins's poetry twenty years ago, but as I read more of his work, I noticed a common structure in most of his poems. His poems begin with something commonplace—snarky or silly or just plain *real* observations about life's moments. By the end, each poem leaves us in a much deeper place, a musing that may be miles away from that original mundane moment.

For example, one of my favorite Billy Collins poems, "I Chop Some Parsley While Listening to Art Blakey's Version of 'Three Blind Mice,'" deftly moves from the literal situation of its title to an imaginative musing about how three mice all came to be blind; then it shifts into a meditation on our universal struggle to reconcile cynicism and sentimentality.

It was not until years later that I heard Billy Collins identify and name this pattern in his own work. Collins (2016) speaks of developing "rhetorical momentum." In a *New Yorker Poetry Podcast* interview with Paul Muldoon, Collins talks about poems as paths toward a point of arrival or "an experience of discovery" at the end. He hopes that discussion of poetry in the classroom can revolve less around the question "What does this poem mean?" and more around "*How* does the poem *go*?"

This becomes particularly noteworthy as we teach students to write narrative pieces. "How does the story go?" is the key question, which is to say, "How does the story move from Point A to Point B?" Sometimes in student writing we see plot that simply plods; their narratives may lack the kind of propulsion readers deserve. What has the writer, in a personal narrative, gained from the experience? Why should a reader care to read about that?

Young adult novelist Jeff Zentner is an expert at this kind of development in his books; notice how his poem "The Shell" provides an excellent model for students who need to move from "what happened" to "why it mattered" in their storytelling.

THE SHELL

by Jeff Zentner

When I was in kindergarten,
the snail in the classroom aquarium died
and my teacher, knowing
that I loved shells for reasons
I could have never articulated
then, gave it to me.

I put it in my backpack and ran
home as fast as I could,
sweating, my blood hungry
for air in the suffocating May heat.

I opened my backpack to show
my mother my prize and found nothing
left of the shell but an assembly
of shards, stinking of water.

This was when I learned
that beauty is fragile.

I think on it still
sometimes: the shell, a hard,

smooth spiral in my small and eager
hand. That I was able
to hold it for a while,
perfect and whole.

This is when I learn
that beauty is also not fragile;
that I am not a graveyard
for everything I have broken.

Reprinted by permission of the author from *The Gospel of Winds*, © 2021.

PRO TIP

If you need to scaffold this kind of strategy a bit more, try substituting a children's poem that demonstrates this same kind of movement, using Scaffolding Strategy 4 in Appendix A.

Students often write narratives that follow the arc of the first three stanzas of the poem, but sometimes they lack the "rhetorical momentum" to move to the depth it plumbs in that fourth stanza. And many, many students will not keep ruminating on the meaning of an experience until they reach those notes of absolution in the final stanza: "I am not a graveyard/for everything I have broken."

Students *can* explore those depths in personal narrative writing. Poetry gives us a way to quickly demonstrate what that movement from plot to reflection, Point A to Point B, looks like in just a short bit of class time. It provides a necessary push.

My first major writing assignment of the school year is usually a narrative, the "Autobiography of a Reader," in which students revisit reading memories and retell those formative experiences. When it comes time to talk about what Nancie Atwell calls the "So what?" of those memories, I tell students, "You may not know when you start writing this piece why a book from childhood rings in your memory so loudly, but when you write, as you show what it looked and felt like to encounter this book, listen quietly for that movement from the *what* to the *why*, the showing to the telling, the imagery of your reading experience to the reflection upon its impact. Our Point A is descriptive narration telling a positive or negative reading memory. Our Point B is reflection: What does this moment mean to us now, and why does it matter?"

Lauren's "experience of discovery" in her Autobiography of a Reader sounded like this:

Through the years, I have found that reading can mean different things for many people. To some people it may act as an escape out of reality, to other people it may just be viewed as a regular pastime, or maybe some people even find it something they dread and cannot begin to enjoy, much less focus on.

For me, in its own way, reading has always felt like a constant. When other people weren't there, the books always were. So yes, I did use it as a way to find other people like me, as well as in the case of *The Dreamer*, a figurative escape, and in the case of *Secret Goldfish*, a literal escape from trouble. In this sense, I feel almost indebted to reading for fulfilling such a large portion of my life.

Not all engines run forever. In fact, they almost always break down at some point. But I hope this engine—reading—never quits on me.

Lauren applies the technique "The Shell" demonstrates, moving into the powerful, reflective content that makes memoir writing sing.

The poem "Big Snow" by Welsh poet Philip Gross provides an example of subtler movement that we can use when helping our students think about the mood they are creating in their narrative scenes.

BIG SNOW

by Philip Gross

the first of the winter, and
people leapt in their cars to meet it,
forging up the moor side till they hit
irrefutable drifts, slewing off at lax angles
anywhere, a festival of rules suspended,

as families came tumbling out, into
the bear hug of whiteness, in their bright
snow clobber—puce, plum, vermilion
swaddlings, mittens, hoods, and puffy boots—
and everyone as pudgy-limbed as toddlers

stumbling off into the stuff at random
gladly, staggered by the revelatory
new land forms—like a high surf
crashing round them that's their friend—
stumbling off but slower now, and now

at a standstill ten yards from the car,
with laughter that was half their body's
fear as the cold struck them speechless,
breath-forsaken, the way it had stroked
every boulder and bush into white-water

stairs such as you'd glimpse in the moment
you drowned—such egregious cold
they trusted it, perversely, like a brawny
uncle back from years "abroad," where
who knows what he does or might have done.

"Big Snow" by Philip Gross. *Poetry*. June-July issue, 2004.

At first glance, this is a free-spirited poem about the transformation and adventure that a big snow brings us. But then there is that last stanza that compares it to the moment of drowning, uses words like "egregious" and "perversely," and alludes to that uncle that resembles a shady character from a black-and-white Hitchcock movie.

What is the poet doing there? Can a moment, a memory, contain both joyful abandon and foreboding danger? It can. The movement in the poem from imagery of bear hugs to white-water drowning captures a shift in mood. Once we help students tune into that in a poem, they can use it to craft more nuanced narrative scenes.

Joy Harjo speaks about to the "ability to travel" that occurs when we write a poem. She says the poet pulls together "strands, patterns, and ideas and then you travel with it. To me that's what's most exciting" (Harjo, 2020, 3:24). We want our students to travel when they write narrative and take their readers along for the ride. Developing this skill as a poet heightens their ability to craft narratives that truly *move,* both structurally and emotionally.

Poems That Demonstrate Narrative Movement Well

1. "Ancestry" by Seán Hewitt

2. "Something You Should Know" by Clint Smith

3. "Sea Dogs" by Eamon Grennan

4. "Revenge" by Taha Muhammad Ali

5. "Summer Storm" by Dana Gioia

6. "Autobiography in Five Short Chapters" by Portia Nelson

7. "testify" by Eve Ewing

8. "Snow Day" by Billy Collins

POETRY PAUSE: CRAFTING A CLIMACTIC TWIST

Poem: "Evening on the Lawn" by Gary Soto

Plan: Students examine how a poet crafts a climactic moment in a poem with an eye on how they might do so in their narrative.

Big Picture: Sometimes storytellers open up a bit of mystery just when the tension in their narrative peaks. Instead of trying to answer every question the reader has and explain it all away, the writer provokes questions. This is a sophisticated skill, so studying it in a short poem before trying it in a longer draft helps us to pinpoint, name, and emulate this sly craft move more quickly than if we waited for the climactic moment in a novel.

When it comes to crafting the climax of a personal narrative, students might rush into the moment or build up to it slowly, even cluttering the climb of the plot with cumbersome details that add nothing. Pausing mid-process to read a full-length mentor text may not be practical, but pausing to let a poem coach us can be. Consider how this poem by Gary Soto can demonstrate a well-paced climb to the climactic moment. It is a snatch of a scene that ends with an unexpected twist, something readers crave in good storytelling.

EVENING ON THE LAWN

by Gary Soto

I sat on the lawn watching the half-hearted moon rise,
The gnats orbiting the peach pit that I spat out
When the sweetness was gone. I was twenty,
Wet behind the ears from my car wash job,
And suddenly rising to my feet when I saw in early evening
A cloud roll over a section of stars.
It was boiling, a cloud
Churning in one place and washing those three or four stars.
Excited, I lay back down,
My stomach a valley, my arms twined with new rope,
My hair a youthful black. I called my mother and stepfather,
And said something amazing was happening up there.

They shaded their eyes from the porch light.
They looked and looked before my mom turned
The garden hose onto a rosebush and my stepfather
    scolded the cat
To get the hell off the car. The old man grumbled
About missing something on TV,
The old lady made a face
When mud splashed her slippers. How you bother,
She said for the last time, the screen door closing like a
    sigh.
I turned off the porch light, undid my shoes.
The cloud boiled over those stars until it was burned by
    their icy fire.
The night was now clear. The wind brought me a scent
Of a place where I would go alone,
Then find others, all barefoot.
In time, each of us would boil clouds
And strike our childhood houses
With lightning.

Even in a short poem, there is still slower pacing as the narrative ascends. The writer emphasizes imagery, not plot, not needless background or true-but-unimportant details. This poem is not a list of little events of the day that lead the critical moment like we sometimes see in student narratives, but a collection of images that takes readers into the speaker's "inner space," capturing his wonder. This invites us to feel what the speaker feels by seeing what he sees.

But then we should ask students, "How does the end of this poem leave you feeling? What does it leave you wondering? What do you want to ask or tell the characters?" The poem is crafted to leave us with questions. It portrays the rift that has occurred between parents and adolescent in this seemingly small moment, but it also intrigues us with what it means to join other "barefoot" comrades and "strike our childhood houses/with lightning."

Challenge students to spin a little bit of that unpredictability, intrigue, shock value, and pathos into the climax of their story. Sell it as more than a turning point. Visualize it as a firework, something incendiary for the characters that will either result in a glorious display of light cascading from the sky or in a missing finger. You've lit the fuse by showing them a poem—now let it ignite in their writing. And while reflection and stepping back from a memory to make sense of it is imperative in memoir and personal narrative writing, make sure our students never feel the pressure to explain everything away. As in Soto's poem, it is OK to leave the reader feeling something deeply.

Poems to Demonstrate a Climactic Twist

1. "Camaro" by Phil Kaye

2. "To a Daughter Leaving Home" by Linda Pastan

3. "Losing My Religion" by Ron Koertge

4. "Young" by Anne Sexton

5. "The Gift" by Li-Young Lee

6. "The Mower" by Philip Larkin

PRO TIP

Need to streamline this poetry pause? Clearly outline the steps you will take before presenting the poem, using Streamline Strategy 4 in Appendix A.

IT ALL COMES DOWN TO THIS

I once had a phenomenal student named Madison compose a narrative ironically titled "I Hate Personal Narratives." She wrote,

> Every year in elementary school, I was forced to construct some pretentious personal narrative. Each time though, my body was overcome with dread, for my demise was in sight. For about three consecutive years I wrote the same. exact. story. It was a poorly constructed tale of how I almost got swept out to sea. Each time I had to write the narrative, a small part of me wished I had been. My teachers always utilized the same ritualistic chant: 'Dialogue! Imagery! Dialogue! Imagery!' I am still convinced that they banged drums on a desert island in their fearsome narrative cult, for I have never witnessed any other human beings so feverish from dialogue.

While it is obvious from the quality of her prose that Madison's teachers succeeded in teaching her to write well, none of us want our students feeling this miserable about a personal narrative assignment! Yet I do not think she is alone.

Many students feel their lives are just not interesting enough to write about. Teachers are encouragers, and we know that is not true. I like how Katherine Schulten put it when encouraging students to tell their pandemic stories for a *New York Times* contest: "Even if you don't think you have something to say, you do. There are stories only you can tell" (para. 5).

Poems can help with this dilemma. They can be encouragers. A student who is accustomed to reading poems already has training in what it looks like to hold a moment up to the light and let its facets gleam, training in how to find what is magical in the mundane. Because poems are less dense than lengthier narratives, we can demonstrate a powerful skill quickly and a student can move on to the business of applying it in their writing.

In Margaret Hasse's poem, "What the Window Washers Did," the window washers break apart "last year's ivy that cast the spell of its thatch across the east windows" and "rubbed the surfaces of all the panes until the glass squeaked and disappeared." What magical powers these cleaners possess! How exciting it is to see lines like these embedded in a student piece of writing as we use poetry to develop their eye for the wonderful and their ear for how to express it.

Jason Reynolds (2017) calls each of the poem-chapters in *Long Way Down*, his masterful novel-in-verse, "tiny elevators on each page that you have to step into and step out of" (1:38:02). Of course, this metaphor fits the plot of this particular book, but it also emphasizes that verse both confines and transports. In the acknowledgments for his book, he goes on to thank "the poets" for "without poetry, especially when I was younger, being a writer would have seemed like a futile attempt. The poets taught me the functionality of language" (1:35:05). That last line resonates through the personal histories, reading, and writing habits of some of the great storytellers in current young adult fiction: Laurie Halse Anderson, Jacqueline Woodson, Jeff Zentner, and Elizabeth Acevedo. Even novelists who never publish in verse are often poets because of the added "functionality of language" practice with poetry gives them. May that be our students' experience as well.

PRO TIP

Do your students love books by Jason Reynolds? Try sharing "Prodigal," a poem from his blog, as an additional mentor for narrative writing, using the QR code below.

POETRY PAUSES FOR ARGUMENT WRITING

My sons were in bed. Gentle water whispered overhead as my wife showered upstairs. The house was quiet, and after a week of hybrid teaching, I was beat. At my dining room table on a Friday night, I took the first opportunity I had to tune into the Dodge Poetry Festival 2020, the largest poetry event in the United States. Of course that year it was a virtual event, streamed and zoomed. I needed something for my mind that did not involve grades, disinfectant, or social distance.

Carolyn Forché read a poem to an online audience of 400 people, telling the story of a Syrian refugee she met repeatedly while taking his cab in wintertime Milwaukee. "He told me his story on the condition that I would write it," she explained (Forché, Espada, & Francis, 2020, n.p.). Martín Espada read a poem about "the two hurricanes that hit Puerto Rico: Hurricane Maria and Hurricane Trump," embedding in his poem the now infamous image of paper towel rolls lobbed into a crowd. Vievee Francis explained how the elegies she writes seek to capture the "keening" that should accompany the loss of each human life, and the sense that this acute loss is muted in a time of pandemic.

In just 30 minutes before dinner, it became clear that all three poets had crafted arguments in their verse: an argument for the dignity of refugees, an argument for the accountability of a leader, an argument for the value and impact of each life lived and lost.

Sometimes I hear teachers and students talk about poetry as if the only purpose for writing a poem is to bare your soul, to go deep and dark; this illuminates another reason why poetry can be such an uncomfortable genre for teachers and students to approach in class. "I just feel funny asking kids to write poems because some of them feel awkward sharing that much of themselves with the world," a teacher told me once.

This view, however, inappropriately confines what poetry can do. No doubt the three poets I quoted earlier are pulling from their deepest feelings, their heart-of-hearts, sharing themselves with the world, but the work they shared that evening was not primarily autobiographical. In fact, I would say it was primarily crafted to make you feel, to the bone, what they felt about an event, an issue, the conditions of the world that affect us all.

Argument embedded in poems is nothing new. Consider the work of nineteenth-century Black poet Frances Ellen Watkins Harper, and her poem "Songs for the People":

SONGS FOR THE PEOPLE

by Frances Ellen Watkins Harper

Let me make the songs for the people,
   Songs for the old and young;
Songs to stir like a battle-cry
   Wherever they are sung.

Not for the clashing of sabres,
   For carnage nor for strife;
But songs to thrill the hearts of men
   With more abundant life.

Let me make the songs for the weary,
   Amid life's fever and fret,
Till hearts shall relax their tension,
   And careworn brows forget.

Let me sing for little children,
   Before their footsteps stray,
Sweet anthems of love and duty,
   To float o'er life's highway.

I would sing for the poor and aged,
   When shadows dim their sight;
Of the bright and restful mansions,
   Where there shall be no night.

Our world, so worn and weary,
    Needs music, pure and strong,
To hush the jangle and discords
    Of sorrow, pain, and wrong.

Music to soothe all its sorrow,
    Till war and crime shall cease;
And the hearts of men grown tender
    Girdle the world with peace.

"Songs for the People" by Frances Ellen Watkins Harper. Originally appeared in *Poems*, George S. Ferguson Company, 1896. Public domain.

After reading this as our poem of the day, I might ask students one or several questions to get them thinking about argument:

- What is she arguing here?

- What need does she identify?

- What stand does she take?

That second-to-last stanza sums it up nicely: "Our world, so worn and weary,/ Needs music, pure and strong." If I do not get a response to my initial questions, I might ask students to identify which stanza contains the main "point" of the poem.

I share that this poet was an abolitionist and a temperance and women's suffrage activist, yet here she pauses to argue that the world needs music. This is a poem of hope, a poem that argues it is important to confront present suffering while also envisioning better things beyond it. It calls for making the music that will help usher in that brighter future. We can certainly read the word *music* figuratively here too: creating harmony, making noise, stirring the heart to action. This is a resonant argument even today.

While argument writing in its other forms—editorial, essay, comic, photojournalism, or speech—must be grounded in fact and reason and eighteenth-century Enlightenment logos, the very best arguments, whatever form they take, also help us to *feel* deeply alongside the writer, to unsettle our complacency or open space for empathy. Poetry lets us bring a little bit of extra pathos, the more nineteenth-century notion of the "wild west wind" that Percy Shelley famously conjures. He begs of that wind, "Drive my dead thoughts over the universe/ Like wither'd leaves to quicken a new birth!" Argument, whether published as a poem or embedded as a bit of verse in the writer's process for another genre, has kinetic energy. It drives away dead thoughts and clears a place for new ones.

POETRY PAUSE: SHARPENING A CLAIM

> **Poem:** a short poem by Rumi
>
> **Plan:** Students craft a claim modeled after a short, memorable poem.
>
> **Big Picture:** This poetic mentor text allows students to think about two facets of their claim: what to do and what not to do. Then it follows up with a metaphorical way of looking at the claim, so before even beginning a draft, students are already thinking about how they might compare ideas and concepts.

My favorite classroom anecdote about the power of poetic claims begins with a bit of poetry from thirteenth-century Persian poet Rumi.

I needed a super short Poem of the Day to share so we could move along with a lengthier lesson, and I chose this little snippet of verse:

> Raise your words
> not your voice.
> It's rain that grows flowers,
> not thunder.

Public domain.

My student, whom I will call Mike to preserve his privacy, angled his tall torso back in his chair and abruptly said, "Wow! I love that one!"

Mike was not a student known to do this. He was a caring friend to his peers with a reputation for being polite. He was also known for a casual attitude toward academic work and often viewed deadlines, even entire assignments, as optional. So his sudden engagement caught my interest even more when he said, "Can I write it down to keep?"

"Sure, Mike!" I said and carried on with our planned brief discussion about what the poet means and how the metaphor enhances that meaning.

A week later came the real shock. The door flew open, shaking our modular classroom a little bit, and Mike entered, just before the bell as the rest of the class was settling in. "I have to tell you something!" he announced, loud enough for everyone to hear. "I used a poem yesterday!"

"That's great . . ." I said, half distracted with attendance-taking. "Have a seat and you can tell us about it."

He began, "So my mom and dad were getting mad at each other about something last night, and they were starting to argue, you know getting louder and angrier. And that poem we did a few days ago popped in my head, about the rain and the thunder."

Suddenly I felt my eyes widen just a little bit as I began to fast-forward. *Uh oh! Where is this story going? Did he quote this poem to his parents mid-argument??? Because my first thought here is that this is a good way to get both parents to turn on a kid, right? I mean, who wants to hear Rumi when you're fighting with your spouse?*

"So I said to them," he continued, "Mom, Dad: 'Raise your words not your voice. It's rain that grows flowers, not thunder.' And it worked. They stopped and we all sort of talked about it."

I paused, tentative. "About the poem?"

"Yeah! And how it means you get farther talking about things calmly like rain instead of loudly like thunder."

I should stop here to say that I still think the more common outcome of quoting poetry to an angry parent would be far less positive, so this story will stick with me for my entire career. A succinct argument in verse written centuries ago had instantaneous relevance in a household dispute, and a fourteen-year-old knew it could. It presented an argument that stopped the other kind of argument, the more painful kind, in its tracks. Wow. Just, wow.

Of course, not all argument writing negotiates family peace. Some is meant to stir us up, to motivate readers, to poke at our conscience and provoke action. Willie Perdomo (2020) refers to the "lyrical machete" a poem can wield (p. 1). There is a sharpness to a good argument, an edge, a ferocity, a danger. And like a machete, it can open a new path through our viny, wild, confusing world. We want students to feel this as they craft argument pieces, but too often they end up recycling opinions they have already heard in words others have used to make the same point. They may shy away from taking a stand, sometimes because they lack a thorough understanding of a topic, sometimes because they lack a real passion for it, and sometimes because they want to avoid being divisive.

A simple poem like Rumi's verse can provide a mentor for sharpening a claim into a few words and a single figurative image. Look at how the poem moves.

Line 1: Do this (Raise your words)

Line 2: Not this (not your voice).

PRO TIP

If your class needs additional support, try turning this poem into a fill-in-the-blank challenge, using Scaffolding Strategy 2 in Appendix A.

Lines 3–4: Here's a metaphor to make that point visual (It's rain that grows flowers,/ not thunder).

This format could be used to write about any topic. Instead of just using this particular poem when I need something quick, I now use it to help us sharpen our claims.

"So think about that format," I tell my students. "Let's see how this pattern could work for your topic. Tell someone what to do and what not to do. Maybe it's replacing an old habit with a better one, like this poem. Maybe it's choosing the tougher-but-better path instead of the easy-but-problematic one."

I continue, "Then comes the trickier part. Can you make this visual with a metaphor? See how it's that last twist that makes Rumi's poem so memorable and enduring? If you disagree with his point at first, the imagery in that metaphor makes it clear . . . yeah, gentleness *can* coax good results, whereas loud thunder doesn't really make anything grow or make anything better. It just thunders, making lots of noise. Try to imagine a quick, simple scenario that fits your topic and does the same."

Once students have had a few minutes to give this a try, ask them to share in a group of four so that they hear three other variations on this model written around three other topics.

"Of course, this is not going to work directly as a claim for your essay," I continue. "But there are some bits we can use here. The poem is short but potent and it gets its point across without muddying it up with lots of words. In fact, it states the main point in just a few words. Let's see if we can do that with our claims."

After students draft a claim to develop, we address the other part of the poem. "The second half is really just a metaphor. But metaphors work just as well in essays as they do in poems. Look at your metaphor. Would you see this as something you could use in the beginning of your essay to pique a reader's appetite for your ideas? Or does it develop a point so well that it belongs in the heart of the essay to make some key evidence stand out? Or is this metaphor so close to your main point that it really needs to be in the last line or two, that final, memorable image to lock the point in your reader's mind? Jot the idea for where this *might* go in your writer's notebook. And remember, it's OK to change your mind later."

Writing a claim does not have to be intimidating, and it is not too early to consider what imagery or figurative language might complement that claim right from the outset of an argument writing project. Students may leave this activity with the sense that they have uncovered something clear and beautiful, which can give them energy for the work ahead: developing support for their claim.

POETRY PAUSE: EMPHASIZING KEY EVIDENCE

Poem: "A Small Needful Fact" by Ross Gay

Plan: Memorable and important facts, however small, can impact an audience and open up a new line of reasoning in argument.

Big Picture: When writers discover a fascinating small fact, it empowers them to go deeper, to elaborate, and to integrate imagery in their argument writing. This skill awakens the curiosity and wonder of both the writer and the reader and moves us away from simply listing facts in support of a claim.

Ross Gay's poem "A Small Needful Fact" spotlights the power and importance of a single detail from a person's lived experience. In this case, that person is Eric Garner, who died in an illegal chokehold while under arrest in Staten Island, NYC. Here is the poem:

A SMALL NEEDFUL FACT
by Ross Gay

Is that Eric Garner worked
for some time for the Parks and Rec.
Horticultural Department, which means,
perhaps, that with his very large hands,
perhaps, in all likelihood,
he put gently into the earth
some plants which, most likely,
some of them, in all likelihood,
continue to grow, continue
to do what such plants do, like house
and feed small and necessary creatures,
like being pleasant to touch and smell,
like converting sunlight
into food, like making it easier
for us to breathe.

"A Small and Needful Fact" by Ross Gay from Split This Rock's *The Quarry: A Social Justice Poetry Database*. 2015.

The poem is simple, elegant, and chilling all at once. In covering the viral popularity of this poem, *PBS News Hour* noted that "much of the press surrounding Garner has focused on the violence of his death, while the poem puts a needed spotlight on his life." While his words, "I can't breathe" have become ubiquitous in our world as awareness of and protest against police violence grows, writer Ross Gay noted, "What the poem, I think, is trying to do is to say, there's this beautiful life, which is both the sorrow and the thing that needs to be loved" (Segal, 2015, para. 3).

PRO TIP

Want your students to write a short argument poem around a small fact? Try writing your own exemplar first, using Scaffolding Strategy 5 from Appendix A!

And so the needful fact around which he crafts the poem is not so small after all. Instead, it is profound evidence supporting the argument that police violence demands society's attention, that those who breathe must speak for those who cannot. It contributes to a broader argument too, that each human life has value and beauty that we cannot allow anything to overshadow. As John Donne put it way back in 1624, "No man is an island."

Students can learn the value of small facts in building an argument. Since poems are small, they give us a good sort of space to practice this skill, but even in longer forms, student writing stands out when the writer has learned the value of well-chosen evidence.

For example, the anthology *Student Voice: 100 Argument Essays by Teens* (Schulten, 2020) has gathered some of the best argument writing by young adults, pieces that lack some of the polish of a professional journalist's work but have the same good bones of excellent opinion pieces from *The New York Times*.

As I read through this trove of mentor texts to share with students, I realized that the essays that kicked around in my head long after reading them were the essays that employed the same tactic Ross Gay used in his poem. They found a tiny thread of a larger issue and teased it out. Then, the writer examined how that small fact was emblematic of a bigger issue and expanded their ideas from there.

For example, one essay was called "I'm a Heterosexual Male Who Wants to See Men in Speedos." What a title! This piece argues that we need to stop objectifying women's bodies, but the writer begins with this small fact: The *Sports Illustrated* Swimsuit Issue has never featured a male body. Another essay argues that the structure of traditional school can erode a student's self-worth, but it studies this through the lens of one common practice: the alphabetical seating of students. At first glance, the broader psychological issue seems to have not much to do with this minutia of school life, but line by line, thread by thread, the author reveals that it does. As a reader, I become intrigued, more engaged in the argument, all starting with a small fact.

Scan this QR code to hear Abel John read and talk about his award-winning argument essay, "Collar the Cat!"

Of the twelve first-place winners in a recent student editorial contest from *The New York Times* Learning Network, the only one I can remember sitting here as I write this, had this same feature. It was Abel John's (2020) editorial about the importance of collaring cats, because—here is something I never knew—songbirds can see color while rodents cannot. So a brightly colored collar on a cat protects native songbirds from invasive predatory housecats while never impeding the cat's ability to control rodent populations. That tiny fact about a tiny adjustment the author believes all cat owners can make to protect songbirds made that argument piece stand out.

To practice this skill in poetry before transferring it into essays, editorials, or researched argument pieces, I share Ross Gay's poem with them. "See how potent and poignant a little detail can be!" Then I use some of these questions to dive in a little more:

- What does this small needful fact add to the argument that a newspaper article could never quite capture?

- How does it give a face to the news?

- How might this background detail about Eric Garner make someone stop and think about the issue of police brutality?

- How does it tug at both your head and your heart?

Next, I present a small fact that relates to a current hot topic, but it is the kind of detail students probably have not come across in broader news coverage of a topic. The "Harper's Index" section at the beginning of some issues of *Harper's Magazine* are excellent for finding these. So is the random fact generator from Mental Floss. So are Snapple caps.

Here are three facts I found in Harper's Index, March 2022:

- TikTok videos tagged #MentalHealth have been watched 25,100,000,000 times.

- Seven out of ten pet owners in the United States say they take their pet's health more seriously than their own.

- 92 of the 100 most-watched TV broadcasts last year were NFL games.

Using one of these facts, I might ask students, "Let's try writing a poem about this fact. I want you to get the reader thinking about a bigger issue here, but the poems must be mostly rooted in this one fact. What does the fact reveal? Does it require emotion or action from the reader? How can your poem bring that to the surface?"

Max, a high school senior, wrote the following poem in response to the TikTok fact mentioned earlier.

SPEAK AND BE HEARD

Tik Tok
Goes the clock
Every hour that passes
Another person joins the masses

We all need help
and so we send out a
cry

#Mental Health
Goes out into the world
A Tik Tok tag captioned
25.1 billion watched

We all go through lots
In each of our own homes
   Little Pods
     Little Biomes

We think we are alone
Even though we ain't
Send something to the web
and you'll see

The whole world is struggling
  even you and me

  You aren't alone
so don't be
   afraid
    to
     shout
Here's the # Spill it out

There is rumination in this poem. Max has not just acquired a fascinating fact; he's mulled it over, given it some thought. This results in discoveries that can be helpful in his essay draft. A few thoughts that might find such a home later in his process:

➤ We each live in our own "little pods/ little biomes."

➤ We are less alone than we imagine, for "the whole world is struggling."

➤ We use social media to "send out a cry" and hashtags allow us to "spill it out."

Next I might ask, "Now what do you want your reader to conclude about social media? What will you claim and argue to be true?"

Students can research an article or two to expand their knowledge of the single fact they started with. My student Jason did this and began expanding his fact into an essay. Here's what it sounds like at that stage of the process:

Fact: 14% of people fighting the California wildfires are prisoners.

While this may seem like a ridiculous and unsafe number, it is more beneficial to prisoners and society than them staying in jail. One reason why the California Department of Corrections and Rehabilitation (CDCR) should maintain and expand this program would be the opportunity it offers those who are qualified. The prisoners currently serving in the fire department have minor offenses, less than five years left in jail, and are on a voluntary basis. This ensures that both the public and prisoners are in safe hands. Besides the prisoners being "safer," they also have other benefits, like having something to put on their résumé when they get out of jail, earning $3 to $5 per hour on the job, and "can also earn time off their sentence by working in the fire camps" (Escalante). This is an opportunity that the prisoners could not have if they were confined in jail.

As his essay continued, Jason went on to examine the potential benefits to firefighting while serving time and present the counterarguments some may raise. For example, some might point out, "They are being paid so little for such dangerous work!" while others might contend, "But prison is supposed to be punishment. Should society give such important work to people who have already broken society's rules in some serious way?" Jason addressed these as he moved ahead with his draft.

Of course, no strong argument can pitch its tent on a single riveting fact. Gay's poem demonstrates this too. It moves from the fact that Eric Garner once worked for the Parks and Recreation Horticulture Department, to the gentleness that this implies, to the way one life can impact a whole ecosystem of lives. From there, it moves to the cruel irony that nurturing these plants made it easier for others to breathe.

These moves heighten the impact of the central argument: Each individual life has beauty that affects others. The second implied argument, given the subject of the poem, is that injustices against individuals also affect us all.

This is complicated terrain, and students will not be able pull off this kind of nuance quickly in their notebooks. Our goal in the classroom, however, is not to create a poem that rivals Gay's original. Rather, we are inviting students to learn from what he is *doing* in the poem, to learn how to unfold a piece of evidence, look at its implications, and connect it to all the supporting ideas a small fact can expose. Their argument writing in any genre will grow with their ability to do this.

POETRY PAUSE: INVITING MULTIPLE VOICES

Poem: "Gatsby Nears 100" by Brett Vogelsinger

Plan: Contrapuntal poetry helps readers and writers think about the counterarguments someone might bring to an idea.

Big Picture: Perspective-taking is a critical skill in many real-life situations, but when we write argument this skill comes to the fore. Never will writers craft an argument assuming everyone easily agrees with them, so they need to be able to see it from other perspectives and address the needs and concerns of other voices to craft an argument that might persuade others to change their thinking.

None of us would want the writers in our care to craft arguments that only examine support for their chosen side of an argument. The world is full of that kind of thinking already. It is too easy. Our students have plenty of models of people launching arguments into echo chambers and failing to examine additional evidence and complexities of an issue.

Crafting good argument means listening to other voices, hearing opposing viewpoints, and countering them sensitively, thoughtfully, and with evidence.

Or, as the Common Core Standards for Writing put it, students must "develop claim(s) and counterclaims fairly, supplying evidence for each while pointing out the strengths and limitations of both in a manner that anticipates the audience's knowledge level and concerns" (Common Core State Initiative, 2010, p. 45). Thinking through counterclaims and counterarguments is a challenging step for most writers. We ask young students, who are new to even their own opinions, to navigate multiple voices on a topic, to negotiate with ideas that oppose their own.

One poetry book I think everyone should read cover to cover is *Olio* by Tyehimba Jess. In his book, Jess resurrects Black musicians from the past and writes in their voices. He often uses contrapuntal poetry in two columns. Each column is from a different speaker's point of view, and the poems weave these musicians' perspectives with the prevailing racist perspectives of the day. About this contrapuntal form, the poet writes,

> On one side, you may have a slave, and on another side, you may have a master, but they have an equal number of syllables . . . (Jess, quoted in Marshell, 2016, para. 18)

> I felt like it's always interesting to get as many sides of a story as you can. A contrapuntal poem has the capability of bringing two people together and having them talk in a way that is very hard to duplicate. It provides a direct back-and-forth; each line informs the other line. That lends itself to a lot of the relationships that I was observing. (Jess, quoted in Marshell, 2016, para. 15)

In short, this form weaves two different opinions, often an argument and a counterargument.

Scan this QR code to read two contrapuntal poems from *Olio*.

To keep things simple, I like to call these poems in two voices "volleyball poems" when I ask my students to write their first-ever contrapuntal poem. It sounds approachable. Like many of the poems I include in this book, the purpose in writing one is not to craft a magnificent verse but rather to use the beauty and focus of a verse to channel our students into richer thinking and better writing. So do not feel like these volleyball poems require a substantial time commitment. They simply require a certain comfort level with poetry and a willingness to play with an idea.

I tell students, "Draw a line down the middle of your page. This is going to act like a volleyball net. You stand on one side of the net, and in that narrow space on your notebook page, write a short poem that shares the essence of what you want to say in your argument essay in only 15 lines. It should look like a poem with line breaks, not just a small essay written into a narrow space. But it doesn't have to be an amazing poem. We are most concerned with getting our thinking down to a few focused words so we don't get swamped later."

Students complete this step and we may take a minute to share our opening serves with a conference partner. Then I continue: "OK, so on the other side of your net is your opponent. This is a person who believes the exact opposite of what you believe. They don't agree with you at all. And if this were volleyball instead of poetry, they'd be looking to spike the ball directly to the ground on your side to score a point. Now what would *they* say about this topic? How would their thinking be different? How would they oppose your ideas? Let's do a second quick draft from this person's point of view in 15 lines or less on the other side of the 'volleyball net' in your notes."

Sometimes, this is all we have time for. The poems serve their purpose of quickly and briefly getting two sides of a matter down on paper. This can prepare us to face the two central questions of counterargument:

➤ What would you say back to your opponent to counter their ideas or assuage their concerns?

➤ How can you build that into your argument as you write it?

In a more advanced class or a group of students who seem pretty engaged by creative writing, you might add another layer to this piece before moving on to your argument essays. Challenge students to revise the poem so that it can become a true "contrapuntal poem." Contrapuntal poems are cleft straight down the middle of each line, just like the original quickly written version, but they can also be read in two different ways, either as two separate columns (on either side of the net) *or* as one poem (crossing the net line-by-line, horizontally). The poem engages argument and counterargument in the same space AND creates interwoven meaning too.

Here is one I wrote using lines from two different 1925 negative newspaper reviews of *The Great Gatsby,* lifted word-for-word in the left column of the poem. I interweave in my right-column response the elements of the book that endure, at least in my mind, long after having read the book. You can read it as two parallel poems OR read each line horizontally.

GATSBY NEARING 100

One finishes	this American novel
Great Gatsby with a feeling of regret	a song of frustration,
not for the fate of the people in the book,	borne ceaselessly into the past
but for Mr. Fitzgerald	immortalized
At the moment	we doubt the promise of impossible dreams
its author seemed a bit bored and	the green light
tired and cynical	at the end of the pier
There is no ebullience here	shimmering
nor is there any mellowness	tempering the wasteful ennui
or profundity. For our part, *The Great*	questions we ask
Gatsby might just as well be	our 2020s world
called *Ten Nights on Long Island*	feeling lost

Both of the original reviewers (first stanza from *The Dallas Morning News* and the second from the *St. Louis Dispatch*) make arguments that have not stood the test of time even though some high school readers might agree with them (cited in Reach, 2013). On my side of the contrapuntal, I counter each argument by changing it with a list of enduring images and relevant ideas from the book. Read together, they create an intriguing juxtaposition. Writing this poem clarified my own thinking about not only what I love about this book but also what I hated about it the first time I read it in high school.

Poems in two voices help our students to contemplate the views of others who think differently from them and may oppose their argument. This can strengthen the writer's resolve and the evidence they bring to build an essay or editorial having already grappled with another's point of view.

POETRY PAUSE: EXAMINING MULTIPLE CHOICES

> **Poem:** "Alley Violinist" by Robert Lax
>
> **Plan:** Reading and writing poems in the structure of multiple-choice scenarios help students to think through possibilities and outcomes related to their topic.
>
> **Big Picture:** Rather than zeroing in on finding the just-right facts to prove a point, excellent writers of argument broaden their approach and engage with ideas that might challenge their claim or provide alternate solutions. This adds depth to the argument. Multiple-choice poems open a door to this kind of thinking.

While poems in more than one voice can be intricate, multiple-choice poems can be straightforward. And sadly, multiple-choice thinking is already a comfort zone for our over-tested students. The good news is that crafting a quick multiple-choice poem to enhance our argument writing is far more fun than answering a multiple-choice question on a standardized test!

Consider the Robert Lax poem, "Alley Violinist." It may be the perfect Poem of the Day because it is short, gets better on a second read, and sparks classroom conversation.

ALLEY VIOLINIST

by Robert Lax

if you were an alley violinist

and they threw you money
from three windows

and the first note contained
a nickel and said:
when you play, we dance and
sing, signed
a very poor family

and the second one contained
a dime and said:
i like your playing very much,
signed
a sick old lady

and the last one contained
a dollar and said:
beat it,

would you:
stand there and play?

beat it?

walk away playing your fiddle?

The poem seems simple at first, but students can make a good case for each of the choices.

Some of my students argue, "Stand there and play! Don't give that entitled jerk what he wants. Play louder for the poorer people! You are bringing them joy." A few particularly entrepreneurial students even say, "Hey, maybe if you stick around you'll get an even bigger payment to go away!"

Others argue, "I don't know, doesn't it make sense to leave and play somewhere else? That guy sounds really annoyed. Why turn this into a bigger conflict. Maybe your violin playing isn't even that great, and bad violin playing sounds really bad!"

And still others like to point out, "Doesn't the third choice let you stay true to yourself and those who love your music and still avoid annoying anyone?"

PRO TIP

The conversation around this poem gets even better with a "Think, Pair, Share" strategy, described in Scaffolding Strategy 3 in Appendix A.

Once students have a claim that they plan to argue with some evidence, challenge them to write a quick multiple-choice poem around their topic like this one.

"So Owen here is planning to argue that we need to improve the food selection in our school cafeteria and bring in more food that students will actually eat and enjoy. He noticed that a lot of kids don't end up eating much at lunch because the selection isn't that good. Let's try to write a poem like this about Owen's topic. Something like . . ."

Now the fun begins, as I create a model for Owen's argument on the whiteboard or under the document camera:

> If you were sent to school with lunch money
>
> And the cafeteria provided three options:
>
> A withered cheeseburger
> A salad with only three bits of iceberg lettuce
> A walking taco in a bag of Doritos
>
> Would you:
>
> Eat the cheeseburger, forcing it to taste like a Whopper in your imagination?
>
> Start a petition for better meals that do more than check a box?
>
> Or skip lunch altogether, saving the money for something else?

The options are slightly madcap and ridiculous, and that is intentional. I say to my students, "Now, I don't know if these are really Owen's options. These may seem a little bit silly. And for some of you, a fourth option might be 'Just pack a lunch from now on!' But when we make ourselves write something out in a short multiple-choice frame like Robert Lax's poems, it does make us think about possibilities. We begin to see a variety of approaches. It's like we refract light through a prism and follow the lines it travels. It's not like the multiple-choice questions on tests that want you to find the single right answer. Instead, these open up multiple possibilities. Try it! It's fun. You might even laugh. But it will make you think of your topic in a different way that helps you to write about it."

In Eric Gansworth's memoir-in-verse, *Apple, Skin to Core* (2020), his poem "Hunger Test 1" uses a multiple-choice structure to look at food in a different way. The list of choices from "a) lettuce and mayonnaise sandwiches" to "d) Bisquick dumplings + chicken wing meat" serve as an ironic way to emphasize the lack of choices families living in poverty have when feeding their family, the compromises parents make to stretch their food supplies to the end of a month (Gansworth, 2020, p. 62). Sometimes when we have to structure an idea in this format, we realize how narrow or painful the options are for responding to a situation.

Formulating a short poem out of several choices can help a student who is stuck skimming the surface of an argument find a way into a new paragraph, a second angle, or a deeper dive. Their argument writing improves as a result, no matter what finished form it takes.

A Word on Transitions

While we may still need to work with students on transition words and phrases to create cohesion, often I see transitions idolized in writing lessons, leaving students with the impression that sprinkling "moreover" or "in addition" throughout their writing will be enough to make a piece cohesive.

In reality, most students need to spend time thinking through their claims, reasons, evidence, and counterclaims more deeply so that they have some meaningful content for transitions to bring together. They need to conceptualize how their bits of evidence connect to each other.

A student writer who thoroughly thinks through their argument piece rarely needs intensive focus on their transitions. A dash of colorful transition words in weak content leaves the reader of an argument feeling disappointed and hollow.

POETRY PAUSE: SPOKEN WORD POEMS AS MODELS AND MENTORS

Poem: spoken word poems from YouTube

Plan: Watch a series of spoken word poems, paying attention to how the writer-performers bring fire to their arguments.

Big Picture: Hearing the way an argument builds and gathers momentum as it presents evidence can give our students an exciting backdrop for writing in this genre. Spoken word poems capture and hold our students' attention, bringing a different and more youthful kind of mentor text into our study of argument.

Getting students to watch the *Button Poetry* channel on YouTube is never a hard sell. The spoken word poets in these videos are consummate performers who add dimension to their words with gesture, voice, and facial expression. These elements amplify the powerhouse arguments embedded in their poems, pulling my students in to listen more keenly to their words. Often, after introducing them to a poet on this site, students will go back on their own and explore the poet's other work after hours. They give themselves some YouTube "homework" I never even assign!

Since not all of the content on
Button Poetry is appropriate for
all classrooms, be sure to preview
the videos first. The channel does
have a playlist of "Classroom-
Friendly Poems."

In the following chart, I offer several poems from this YouTube channel that show the many faces of argument in the world of contemporary spoken word poetry. This is just scratching the surface of what's available, so preparation is key. The questions column provides possible directions you could take with each of these poems, but of course these are not exhaustive possibilities.

Poem	Topic	Questions	QR Code
"When We Were Kings" by Rachel Wiley	Gender Stereotypes	What is Rachel Wiley's central argument in this poem? Which lines make this argument most impactful?	
"Ten Responses to the Phrase 'Man Up'" by Guante	Gender Stereotypes	What common phrases do you hear people use that express underlying stereotypes? In his argument, what does Guante reveal are the costs of telling boys to "man up?"	
"Totally like whatever, you know?" by Taylor Mali paired with "Like Totally Whatever" by Melissa Lozada-Oliva	Language and Power	What argument is Mali making? What do you agree or disagree with in this argument? How does Lozada-Oliva counter this argument in her poem?	
"Complainers" by Rudy Francisco	Hardship and Loss	How does Francisco support his argument that people complain too easily and too often? Why are the specific details in his evidence more powerful than sweeping broad statements?	

Poem	Topic	Questions	QR Code
"cuz he's black" by Javon Johnson	Racism	What is Johnson's central argument in this poem? How does using small narrative introduce an argument in this poem? What lies have you heard adults tell children?	
"Camaro" by Phil Kaye	Memory and Loss	What is something worth splurging on? What is a decision you made in your life that you will remember forever?	
"Explaining My Depression to My Mother" by Sabrina Benaim	Mental Health	In this poem, Benaim catalogues several common "solutions" loved ones may offer to someone with depression. How does she counter each solution?	

Remember, it is also OK to share spoken word poetry with a class simply for the purpose of letting them hear what impassioned, well-defended arguments sound like, without explicitly analyzing each of the poems. For example, as we are deep in the writing process of an argument piece, I might simply use five spoken word poems as my Poems of the Day that week, and tell my students on Monday, "In each of these poems, I want you to hear and feel the *fire* that these writers bring to their topics and the way they use words to make you feel that fire too. All good argument does that, whether it's an essay, a poem, a book, or a song. Let's keep that in front of us all week: Let your audience feel your fire."

If you need to isolate one aspect of argument writing from one or a series of spoken word poems, consider listening to a few with your class and particularly attending to the conclusions. These conclusions are often built to be "mic drop" moments, words to bring the audience to cheers.

Many of the written standards we apply in our classrooms rather drily refer to students learning to write "a concluding statement or section that follows from and supports the argument presented." But without a truly moving model, we know most students fall back into that uninspired habit of "tell 'em what you told 'em" or "summing it up" in their closing lines. These poems teach them that there are far better, more inspiring ways to close an argument.

IT ALL COMES DOWN TO THIS

If we are not careful, students may only read and write arguments once a year during a unit on this topic. Sharing arguments in poetic form helps expose our students to more frequent, varied arguments in surprising and innovative forms. In my classroom, spoken word poems and slam champions are a regular part of my Poem of the Day routine, so even when we are not studying argument, I regularly expose my students to passionate reasoning.

When it is time to craft a longer argument piece, poems can help us step away, think about how claims and ideas work, and then get back to our central focus with renewed direction and vigor.

My sons love to play with Lego bricks, and I think that allowing our students to play with argument in poems is a lot like this kind of play. An inexperienced builder may have a vision of what they would like to construct from a bucket of colorful bricks, but their first builds are slipshod and easily broken. From this acquired experience, they begin to learn smarter, stronger ways to build, and over time, a child's original projects become more like the professional kits, built to last.

In the same way, when we give our students varied "bricks" to play with in their notebook, they can start snapping together arguments in amateur but creative ways and develop skills that transfer well to their longer work. They will discover new configurations of words and ideas that lock together well and add strength to an argument, and they will be far better at this with some time to play than they will if we just put an annual argument prompt in front of them and tell them to write.

As English teacher Glenda Funk (2020) puts it, "The elegance of argument lives in poetry" (para. 1). Pausing to think and write in poetic form helps to build our students' awareness of this elegance and helps them generate the kinds of arguments that *move* an audience.

POETRY PAUSES FOR WRITING INFORMATIVE AND RESEARCH PIECES

My first memory of learning formal research writing—notecards, bib cards, bibliography, and MLA format—was eleventh-grade Honors English class with Miss Mathison. This was the infamous "term paper" that had us all quaking in our boots. The assignment was one her students both feared and awed, for Miss Mathison required a fifteen-page research paper on an American novel of our choice. The sheer heft of this project fascinated us and created buzz.

I remember choosing to read *East of Eden* by John Steinbeck and thinking to myself, "Well, at least a book this long will give me plenty to write about!" It did. In the end, I needed to purchase a second 100 pack of 2 × 3 index cards and my paper was closer to thirty pages.

Miss Mathison had a particular magic for bringing dull content to life—somehow she helped me enjoy *The Scarlet Letter* that year—and my memories of this semi-overwhelming paper are mostly fond. There was even some friendly competition between me and my classmates over whose paper was inching into the longest one in the class. Perhaps Miss Mathison's real magic was how she found time to read them all!

Fast forward six years, and I was the teacher, standing in front of a class of eighth graders trying to make research skills lively for them and mostly failing. As I understood it, my primary responsibility was to teach them where to put the period in a bibliographic entry. I neglected to think about how to tap into their wonder, how to scratch at a question that itches, how to present their discoveries in an engaging way to an audience. In our flurry of paper notecards my first year and online notecards by year three, I lost the whole point of *why* humans research and why we should *want* to research a topic in the first place.

Even at the collegiate level, experts find it challenging to balance students' need for organization skills with the authentic researcher's need for investigative wanderlust. I love the title of Professor William Badke's article (2015) titled "Teaching Research Skills: Precise, Linear Path or Messy Jungle Running?" In it he notes,

> Scholars tend not be linear. Thus, determining a research problem may be far along the information-gathering timeline, which creates all sorts of inefficiencies, even if scholars are adding to their knowledgebase as they proceed. . . . The most serious problem with having students do research like the scholars is that students lack the expertise to make it successful. Scholars run through the jungle, inviting chaos because they understand the lay of the land. Students who are thrust into the jungle don't know what they are dealing with. They can't distinguish friend from foe from less-than-helpful acquaintance. (Badke, 2015, p. 72)

In other words, it is tough to have students practice and write research in the same, hunt-and-gather manner as an expert who approaches research with abundant background knowledge. Nonetheless, Badke (2015) does note that instruction in research strategy is becoming more "holistic . . . less of a how-to and more of a what-you-need-to-understand" (p. 71). These changes in best practices allow us more space as we work with our school librarians and our citation guides to help students think broadly. A more holistic approach can help us carve a path with our students through the jungle.

We must remember that research can be naturally motivating to students. Much of what our students know about their favorite celebrities comes from free-time research. My oldest son is a Minecrafter and my younger son is a rollercoaster fanatic, and each will spend hours on YouTube researching those topics if I let them. Many teachers are fond of saying that their best professional development happens during passive research on Twitter; follow the right people and excellent articles find you. And anyway, there are very few new experiences I encounter, from travel to movies to sports, that do not lead me to a Wikipedia page, and sometimes down a rabbit hole in the list of references at the bottom of the page.

Poets are no different. Many poems are created by people who relish research and the distilled presentation of knowledge, observation, analysis, and evaluation of things discovered through research. Amanda Gorman's memorable inaugural poem, "The Hill We Climb" started this way: "Gorman began the process, as she always does, with research" (Alter, 2021, para. 21). Her book, *Call Us What We Carry*, is filled with poems that began this way.

In an essay about the role of research in poetry, Gregory Welch (2020) says, "researching like a poet means collecting eclectic bits of knowledge. Searching for something specific that can improve your poem and bring it to life for your audience" (para. 27). Many times, the finished product we read is only a partial reveal of the discoveries a poet has made in their research process, and the brevity of the poem disguises labor that is more like a journalist, biographer, or historical fiction novelist.

Many renowned modern poets are also accomplished researchers who write in other genres, publishing entire books of well-researched nonfiction.

> *Winter Hours* by **Mary Oliver**: Alongside Oliver's signature musings on geese and dogs and meadows are these well-researched literary analysis essays on Poe, Hopkins, Frost, and Whitman.

> *World of Wonders* by **Aimee Nezhukumatathil**: A blend of memoir and meditations on the natural world in a debut essay collection.

> *How the Word Is Passed* by **Clint Smith**: An examination of the lasting impact of slavery, told through the stories of several American landmarks.

> *Singing School* by **Robert Pinsky** and *How to Read a Poem* by **Edward Hirsch**: Two books to improve your own understanding of poetry through a deep dive into the history and intertextuality of the genre.

Meanwhile, researchers writing book-length nonfiction appreciate the poetic quality of language. Laura Hillenbrand, famous for her well-researched bestsellers *Seabiscuit* and *Unbroken*, says that "good writing has a musical quality to it, a mathematical quality, a balance and a rhythm. . . . You can feel that much better when it's read aloud" (as cited in Larimer & Gannon, 2020, p. 84) She is not talking about poems; she is talking about grand-scale research papers that have successfully engaged broad audiences. Nonfiction writers pay attention to the details of not only what they are saying but also how they say it.

But what does all this have to do with our students? Can pauses for poetry really help them to improve the quality of their research? Veteran high school teacher Jim Burke (2020) notes that research papers present a challenge because "many [students] lack the stamina and attention in the early stages to do such in-depth and sustained work. . . . And yet we must find a way, for it is in these assignments that the greatest opportunity for transformation lie" (p. 134).

In my class, it is not long before students develop the stamina and attention to write a poem, and soon these short bits in the writer's notebook feel more inviting than taxing, more playful than prescriptive. So challenging a student to write a poem that starts with a fact can be a handy first step to drawing a line between their poetry writing and research writing.

Just like in the other chapters in this book, we will also examine here how planned poetry pauses interrupting a lengthier research writing project can help students develop and maintain the stamina and attention required to do well in creating an academic research paper.

POETRY PAUSE: TRANSLATING RESEARCH INTO A POEM

> **Poem:** "Altered Axis" by Amy Boyd
>
> **Plan:** Have students explain some of their research discoveries in poetry.
>
> **Big Picture:** Writing based on research can be profound and moving. Pausing to write some discoveries as poems early in our research writing process helps students learn how to blend fact and feeling in powerful ways they can later use in a research paper.

Sometimes poets create poems specifically inspired by facts and research. Our students can do the same.

Australian writer Alicia Sometimes (2020), in her TEDx talk "Honouring Your Wonder," says "poetry and science have grown up together as siblings; . . . they are closer together than they are apart. . . . When we read a poem, we run to the science books to find out more. When we listen to science or look at the stars, we run inside to write a poem" (0:29).

The poem "Altered Axis" demonstrates this well. It is by Dr. Amy Boyd, a professor of biology, and it captures at once the wonder and the scientific detail of what happens when a tree falls and is consumed by the forest.

ALTERED AXIS

by Dr. Amy Boyd

Five years into decay, the hickory topples,
becomes an altered axis in the forest,
dislodging the branches of others,
crushing tender small neighbors as it lands
crashing onto the duff.

No longer propped against gravity, the bole reclines
on damp humus. Slowly, more and more
gossamer nets of hyphae thread their way
through dimensions of lignin and cellulose, the dead
and the still-living cells of the fallen giant.
Beetles, grubs, termites, millipedes, nematodes
squirm in, eat through, go hunting,
break down, consume, defecate,
and the tree-substance transforms,
becoming bug-substance and soil-substance and
air-substance, energy freed into atmosphere.

A seed lands on the softened wood,
soaks up moisture, swells, opens
and lets go of its tiny embryo
and a new tree begins on the old remains,
building from decay and air and light
new form and substance,
verdant, vital, nubile, persistent,
reaching up, retracing a memory
of the old one's ascent,
life leading out of death
from life crumbled.

From *Consilience*, Issue 8

This poem is beautiful to read, not just because of its imagery, but because of its rich, scientific vocabulary. It might equally appeal to a student of creative writing as to a high school junior in AP Biology. The poem teaches us by helping us visualize and name the details of a biological process.

So if experts in their field can turn to poetry in order to communicate, can we teach our students to do the same? Inviting them to write a poem like this can prepare them to communicate complex scientific ideas from their research in simple, vivid, elegant language.

This same concept works for other disciplines as well.

I once worked on an integrated research project with the history teacher on my eighth-grade team. Students chose a lesser known historical figure from the era they studied (early America through the Civil War) to spotlight in a short research paper.

PRO TIP

Two of my favorite books from my classroom library that model research presented in verse are *Dreams From Many Rivers: A Hispanic History of the United States Told in Poems* by Margarita Engle (2019) and *Carver: A Life in Poems* by Marilyn Nelson (1997).

This type of project is fairly common, and it can be ghastly dry, threatening to swallow your weekend as the papers turn into a blur of facts that leave you dead-eyed on a Sunday evening, just skimming for in-text citation errors.

Can research papers that integrate the content areas actually be fun to read?

After my eighth-grade students completed their research notes in history class but before they started drafting their essays in English class, I invited them to write a series of poems.

We had recently finished independently reading novels-in-verse, chosen by the students, so mentor texts were already at our fingertips. I also shared a few first-line prompts that could get them started writing a persona poem from a historical person's point of view. The full assignment sheet is on the companion website, but some of the starters included "What I remember most . . ." and "My mind is like . . ."

Scan this QR code to visit the companion website and see the directions I shared with eighth-grade students to write a series of poems based on their research.

Slowing down our research project by a day or two to process the research in a creative way, to think of synthesizing it artistically not just academically, allows the facts to percolate. It brews a bit of joy. It allows students to give voice to the ideas they found in their research in words that are lovely. Poetry pauses help our students to examine their research with an artist's eye.

When we help students create a little beauty in their notebooks, it goes a long way in motivating them for what is next, and some of that beauty even finds its way into the final copies we teachers spend our Sunday nights reading.

Here are two poems written by Amy, an eighth-grade student researching Eli Whitney. Notice how this pair of poems make the facts of his life that Amy discovered in her research more vivid and three-dimensional.

DETERMINATION

So interested to see
how that one watch worked,
I lied to my parents
in order to stay home
from church.
I took it apart,
and put it back together
but I had to hold my excitement back
when my sister came home.
I had to hold my tongue,
not tell her.

INTERCHANGEABLE PARTS

Changing the way
life was lived in the day –
that was the thing
that I liked to do.
Soldiers would dread
the long wait
for their
broken weapons
and get through the chill
in the heart
that their weapons
wouldn't be fixed in time.
So I invented
interchangeable parts,
which is something
people still use
as they live, today.

Amy had to imagine an experience from Eli Whitney's early childhood in the first poem and bring to life the "chill/ in the heart" that motivated innovation in the second one. Writing poems nudges students to think about something in a way they might otherwise bypass when taking on a research project. In the same way a bypass saves travel time but avoids the quaint main streets and historical roots of a place, jumping headlong from informational reading to informational writing can sacrifice some memorable discovery in the quest for efficiency. A brief meander into poetry can help.

Poems That Incorporate Research

1. "A Bullet With Your Name on It / *Las Vegas, October 1, 2017*" by Luray Gross

2. "Off-Island CHamorus" by Craig Santos Perez

3. "Plastic Snow" by Sam Illingworth

4. "Meteor Shower" by Clint Smith

5. "Canary" by Rita Dove

6. "It comes through the air – a contrapuntal" by Heidi Williams

POETRY PAUSE: EYE-OPENING IRONY

Poem: "Ozymandias" by Percy Shelley

Plan: Students can keep an eye out for irony as they read research sources, thinking about what appeals to a reader.

Big Picture: Since research writing requires lots of reading, some students struggle with knowing what to extract for their writing. "Ozymandias" gives us an opportunity to talk about why ironies are so memorable and enduring and why they make great content for research writing pieces.

In *The Writer's Practice*, John Warner (2019) talks about teaching his college students to "digest" an article in their research project—"a process that focuses on what you need to meet your objective, rather than digging into every last morsel of information." Then he says students must "translate" that article, and while "keeping your focus on your audience's needs, attitudes, and knowledge, tell them what's up with the research" (pp. 133-134). By encouraging students to think of an audience as they scour their research sources, we prepare them to write engagingly and well.

In nonfiction, research-based writing outside of schools, nothing engages readers like irony. A cruel twist of fate, a surprising contradiction, the triumph against all the odds: this sells books and rivets readers. Knowing this helps students figure out which morsels of information are worth keeping and including in their work. A quick look at a poem can help define the kind of gold we are mining in our research.

Of all the anthologized poems I read in my own high school experience, "Ozymandias" by Percy Bysshe Shelley stands out, and it calls me back occasionally for a re-read. Its survival, both in my memory and in the canon of British literature, has much to do with its delicious irony.

OZYMANDIAS

by Percy Bysshe Shelley

I met a traveller from an antique land,
Who said—"Two vast and trunkless legs of stone
Stand in the desert. . . . Near them, on the sand,
Half sunk a shattered visage lies, whose frown,
And wrinkled lip, and sneer of cold command,
Tell that its sculptor well those passions read
Which yet survive, stamped on these lifeless things,
The hand that mocked them, and the heart that fed;
And on the pedestal, these words appear:
My name is Ozymandias, King of Kings;
Look on my Works, ye Mighty, and despair!
Nothing beside remains. Round the decay
Of that colossal Wreck, boundless and bare
The lone and level sands stretch far away."

Public domain.

A haughty king, who thought he was "King of Kings," is now dead. He is so long dead that even his monumental statue has collapsed to "trunkless legs." The "sneer" on the statue's face is just a "shattered visage." Sharing the image in Figure 5.1, created by eighth-grade student Mackenzie, will help your students accurately imagine the central image of the poem.

5.1. A middle school student's artwork inspired by Shelley's "Ozymandias."

I say, "That last line, wow! 'The lone and level sands stretch away.' It intensifies the theme that no matter how powerful you are, time erodes the 'cold command' of all leaders. That thought has stuck with me from the first time I read this poem in high school!"

"As you read articles in your research, watch for what's ironic like this. Where are the details and facts that surprise you, where are the outcomes that turn out the opposite of how we would expect? When the mighty fall, or the underdog wins, that's intriguing to a reader, that's an idea that sticks. Let's take a look at how some writers take ironic facts and spotlight them in nonfiction writing."

In my own nonfiction reading, some of the points that stick with me long after I finish are the ironies that open my eyes to something unbelievable but true.

From Erik Larson's *Dead Wake*: I recall the irony that Alfred Gwynne Vanderbilt cancelled his scheduled passage on the *Titanic* but later boarded the *Lusitania* and died when it was torpedoed.

From Rebecca Skloot's *Immortal Life of Henrietta Lacks*: I remember that Henrietta Lacks, whose immortal cells revolutionized medicine for all of us, had children who lived in poverty for decades while others made millions of dollars from petri dishes filled with their dead mother's living cells.

From Ben Mezrich's *Woolly*: I discovered that part of the justification for resurrecting woolly mammoths via their DNA is that it will counteract the release of carbon into the atmosphere and preserve humanity.

From John Green's *The Anthropocene Revisited*: I learned that the man who opened Piggly Wiggly, the first supermarket chain, radically altering the way Americans shop for and consume food, went bankrupt twice and died in a sanitorium. And this simple observation about humans from the book rings in my head long after the rest has faded: "We are at once far too powerful and not nearly powerful enough."

Excellent research involves the meeting of fact and feeling, the gathering of ideas from many sources and the presentation of them with insight. "Ozymandias," reminding us of life's ironies, is the perfect poem to start off the research or informative writing unit, as we help our students ascertain what details will engage an audience with stranger-than-fiction facts.

"As you research, keep a special place in your notes for those ironies you find, those unexpected twists. They make for excellent writing later," I tell students. They are ready to read from their sources with a fresh perspective, remembering always their someday readers and what facts will pack the biggest punch.

POETRY PAUSE: FOUND POEMS

Poem: A poem created by Brett Vogelsinger based on a *New York Times* piece and a blackout poem by high school junior Charley.

Plan: Students take a passage from their research reading, copy and paste it, and manipulate the text to transform it into a found poem.

Big Picture: Reading research means noticing the right details. Taking a longer passage and moving its parts around into a found poem highlights which parts are most vital and interesting to use in research writing, training the writer's eyes for keen reading.

Found poetry is approachable to create because it reconfigures words that already exist. For years, my classes only wrote found poems as a kind of curiosity, a filler lesson before a break, or sometimes as an engaging way to key in on the structure of a passage. While found poems can serve these purposes, they can also become magnifying glasses that help students to zero in on what matters most in a research source.

What Researchers and Poets Say About Found Poems

Teacher-writer Lesley Roessing (2019) classifies found poems as a type of writing-to-learn activity, a writing challenge that helps us comprehend and then synthesize key details from a text. In a column for *AMLE* she writes,

> Writing found poetry involves determining the important details in a text and the ways in which perceiving and even recording these details leads to increased comprehension of the text and its meaning. . . . This strategy takes readers through the critical thinking taxonomy of analysis, evaluation, and synthesis and teaches readers to look for and then determine important, not interesting, details. (Roessing, 2019, para. 6)

In their research process, students then need to determine what passages can be discarded as unhelpful, which can be paraphrased, and which should be directly quoted. Psychologists say that on average, people make 35,000 decisions a day, but anyone working on a research project is sure to experience an uptick. Pausing to craft a few found poems can provide valuable practice and help our students find their footing in this work and sort through their research reading successfully.

Of course some found poems create more of a collage out of some of the language in a piece, and these can be useful too, what Roessling (2019) calls a "reformulating" of the original text. This can give students the practice in teasing out and cinching together the most critical bits of a text, examining them closely.

Stephen Dunning and poet William Stafford (1992) see an additional benefit to crafting found poems with children as they develop an eye and ear for style in writing: "This [found poem] exercise gives us a chance to celebrate ordinary prose: its concreteness, its richness, and its surprises. In this exercise we're against fancy language. . . . You can find moving, rich language in books, on walls, even in junk mail" (p. 12).

The simplest, quickest type of found poem to write simply involves lifting an excerpt from a text and breaking it into lines, making it look like a poem, sculpting the same clay into a different shape. A sample I have created to share with my students was taken from a quote from the article "High School Doesn't Have to Be Boring" (Mehta & Fine, 2019). First, we read the quote in its prose form (see Figure 5.2), projected on a PowerPoint slide in the front of the classroom.

5.2 An excerpt from "High School Doesn't Have to Be Boring" (*The New York Times*)

As we spent more time in schools, however, we noticed that powerful learning was happening most often at the periphery – in electives, clubs, and extracurriculars. Intrigued, we turned our attention to these spaces. We followed a theater production. We shadowed a debate team. We observed elective courses in green engineering, gender studies, philosophical literature and more.

As different as these spaces were, we found they shared some essential qualities. Instead of feeling like training grounds or holding pens, they felt like design studios or research laboratories: lively, productive places where teachers and students engaged together in consequential work.

From "High School Doesn't Have to Be Boring" by Jal Mehta and Sarah Fine. *The New York Times.* March 30, 2019.

Then I share my found poem, adapted from this text:

> As we spent
> more time in schools, however,
> we noticed that powerful learning
> was happening
> most often at the periphery
>   — in electives, clubs and extracurriculars.
> Intrigued, we turned our attention
> to these spaces.
>
> We followed a theater production.
>   We shadowed a debate team.
>   We observed elective courses in green
>   engineering,
>   gender studies,
>   philosophical literature
>   and more.
>
> As different as these spaces were,
> we found they shared
> some essential qualities.
>
> Instead of feeling
> like training grounds
> or holding pens,
> they felt
> like design studios
> or research laboratories:
>   lively, productive places
>   where teachers and students
>   engaged together
>   in consequential work.

I think aloud with my students and invite their observations about what happens when we reshape the passage: "So when I take this quote and just sort of break it down differently in my notebook, do you notice any details of what the author is saying? You have to read it differently and tease out the details. When you see the quote written like this, which bits jump out as most important or interesting?"

For me, the list of verbs, "followed . . . shadowed . . . observed," leaps forward, emphasizing that this is action research performed by the writers and their conclusions are based on time actually spent in high schools. My attention to the contrast between "holding pens" and "design studios" is heightened when I arrange the text into a poem.

"Teachers and students engaged together" stands out as a core, significant premise in this piece. These are my observations; students will have others.

Next, it is the students' turn to give this method a try. I tell them, "Go back to a source that you discovered in your research. Skim it for a passage that feels important and useful to your work. Copy it into your notebooks, breaking it into lines so you can see it like a poem. What jumps out at you? What words or phrases are so strong they should be a direct quote? Which pieces fall away and become background to the main point of this quote?"

After they have given this a try, I might say, "Now, we won't have time to do this with every quote we examine for this project. But feel free to do this with a few, filling your notebook pages as you go. And keep looking at key passages this way. Can you mentally start to highlight those key words and phrases that might make it into your direct quotes? That skill helps you to be efficient and focused as a researcher!"

One type of poem that invites students into a more tactile reformulation of a text is a blackout poem. Once a student has identified an online text from a reliable source that promises to provide good ideas for their writing, we can have them print a copy and try turning it into a blackout poem. Like a traditional found poem, blackout poems require students to sift through a text and find the parts that fit together in a new, more minimalist whole, but in this case, they use a black marker and a physical page to make it happen.

Figure 5.3 provides an example from Charley, a high school sophomore.

5.3 Charley's black out poem

Charley's excavation of this article has revealed an important message about creativity. When I look at this, words and phrases like "different angles," "shape and develop," "you must release, submit and adapt" become interesting words worth using in a research paper about how to become more creative. In a conference, I can ask him, "What are you finding in your research that elaborates on how creative people shape and develop ideas? In what other sources are you learning about the importance of adapting when it comes to a creative endeavor?"

A quick search online will yield many images of "blackout poems" to share with your students, but resist the urge to use the most beautiful, artistic blackout poems as exemplars. While these would be noble endeavors at some future point, during a research project, simplicity allows the found poem to do its work: spotlight critical details within an article.

POETRY PAUSE: THE HOW-TO POEM

Poem: "Exercises for a Nature Writer" by Tanya Shadrick (after Wendell Berry)

Plan: Students articulate a process, timeline, or procedure that is important to their research in a "how-to" poem.

Big Picture: Research projects can feel overwhelming, and by asking our students to put important play-by-plays into words succinctly, we make the work more approachable. They discover words and images that can later transfer to a research paper draft.

Writing a tutorial as a poem is not a new idea, and published examples abound. Some include "How to" in the title, some are crafted in a "Step 1, Step 2" format, and still others are structured as recipes. In the inset, I have included several How-To poems worth examining, but for now, let's look at Tanya Shadrick's poem, "Exercises for a Nature Writer." Shadrick is a nature writer, not primarily a poet, but in this piece she captures the kind of observation a person must bring to the world if they want to succeed as a nature writer.

EXERCISES FOR A NATURE WRITER
(AFTER WENDELL BERRY)

by Tanya Shadrick

Rise like a farmer at five,
and sit in kitchen silence.
Shepherd thoughts.

Dress for the weather,
taking pen, paper, pocketknife.
Stay out all day.

Do not forget to eat
with your whole concentration
on eating.

Chew as cows do.
Ruminate.
Let everything be well-digested.

Ask: Are my ears good?
The tendons & intentions
that move my pen?

Work loose what is stuck in you
Through service
To whatever crosses your path.

Inspect the edgelands daily.
Make holes in every fence
For life to slip through.

Printed with permission from Tanya Shadrick.

Shadrick's poem, written after the Wendell Berry poem "How to Be a Poet," uses the command form of verbs, intensifying each line by beginning with an action. Like the found poem and blackout poem, this subgenre of poetry quickly gets to the point and captures the essence of a process or an idea.

Jaden wrote this poem in his notebook in the few minutes of writing time that followed our reading of Shadrick's poem:

EXERCISES FOR A HOCKEY PLAYER
by Jaden

Awake early, for it's a big day.
Play hockey this night: a game to be fought.
Eat a buttered bagel, rich with carbs.
Hydrate, for the water will soon be needed.
Work out, though not too hard.
Rest easy. Recline for the few hours to come.
Drive to the rink. Adjust to the cold.

Sometimes, the research projects we encourage students to pursue are also about a process, procedure, or proposed solution to a problem. It's time to move past the classic how-to writing of yesteryear, "How to Make a Peanut Butter and Jelly Sandwich." There are far more interesting, clever, poetic ways to write directions, as Jaden's poem demonstrates.

These quick, low-stakes, verb-driven poems in their writer's notebooks provide a skeleton for explaining a process or proposal in greater detail. I tell them, "So at this point, you have read from the experts to learn what steps we can take to succeed at something. There is a lot swimming around in your mind right now, and before we start thinking about turning this into a longer piece of writing, let's just try thinking about it as a poem, just like Tanya Shadrick boils down everything a nature writer needs to do into just twenty-one lines."

"Of course, this isn't everything she thinks a nature writer has to do . . . she doesn't even mention writing! But it does capture the essence of the work, the careful observation and thinking skills a nature writer needs to bring to the environment. In about twenty lines of a poem, can you write similar directions to start putting together the process you have been learning about?" This could work equally well for a project on controlling carbon emissions as it can for a project on how the local football team can make it to the Super Bowl. And because the lines tend to start with action verbs, it sets the student up to write with more vivid, active voice when it is time to expand their writing later on.

More How-To Poems

1. "How to Be a Poet" by Wendell Berry

2. "How to Eat a Poem" by Eve Merriam

3. "How to Be a Snowflake" by Elaine Magliaro

4. "Recipe for Joy" by Amy Ludwig VanDerwater

5. "Peace: A Recipe" by Anna Grossnickle Hines

6. "A Digital Land Acknowledgement" by Deirdre Lee

7. "Things to Do in the Belly of the Whale" by Dan Albergotti

8. "How to Be a Mole" by Elaine Magliaro

9. "Pass On" by Michael Lee

POETRY PAUSE: STUDYING STANZAS TO KILL THE FIVE-PARAGRAPH ESSAY

Poem: "Winter Stars" by Sara Teasdale

Plan: By learning about stanzas, students learn to identify where shifts in focus happen within a text and improve the organization of their informative writing.

Big Picture: Students raised on the five-paragraph essay format struggle to sense when paragraphing needs to occur. They may only be able to think about paragraphing when prewriting or outlining. Looking at how poets arrange a poem in stanzas raises their antennae to the organization of ideas within a text.

Why is learning to paragraph so important? Relying on prefabricated paragraphing hamstrings our students' ability to perceive shifts in their own writing. John Warner, author of *Why They Can't Write* (2018), simply puts it this way:

> In reality, every piece of writing is a custom job, not a modular home, and by steering students toward the five-paragraph essay we are denying them the chance to practice real writing by confronting the choices writers must navigate. The five-paragraph essay as employed does not allow students to struggle with the important skills underlying effective writing the same way training wheels don't allow nascent bike riders to practice balance. (p. 29)

The wobbly practice of paragraphing ideas, particularly in a longer, committed project like a research paper, can be uncomfortable to watch. If your students seem conditioned to think in five-paragraph essays or unconditioned to think of paragraphing at all, research writing presents a particular challenge. To train our writer's sense of where these shifts in focus occur, and yet abandon the "training wheels" of the traditional five-paragraph form, the short space of a poem can provide some helpful practice.

Before you can use the method I am about to share, your students need to know the word *stanza*. I often tell students that the stanza is "a paragraph of poetry," so by the time I start using stanza breaks to teach paragraph breaks, this casual metaphor is familiar to them.

Let's look at these two definitions from *Merriam-Webster.com* side-by-side:

> **stanza**: a division of a poem consisting of a series of lines arranged together in a usually recurring pattern of meter and rhyme

> **paragraph**: a subdivision of a written composition that consists of one or more sentences, deals with one point or gives the words of one speaker, and begins on a new usually indented line (Merriam-Webster, n.d.).

So, where do these concepts overlap? Division. Stanzas and paragraphs divide ideas to help readers see and understand them in a certain way desired by the author.

Sara Teasdale's poetry is wonderful for many reasons, but her lovely poem "Winter Stars" makes it easy for students to see how stanzas divide a larger idea into sections that shift focus as they move. For some background knowledge, I share that this poem was written in response to World War I, which my students study in their history class, and that Orion is a well-known constellation of stars.

WINTER STARS

by Sara Teasdale

I went out at night alone;
 The young blood flowing beyond the sea
Seemed to have drenched my spirit's wings—
 I bore my sorrow heavily.

But when I lifted up my head
 From shadows shaken on the snow,
I saw Orion in the east
 Burn steadily as long ago.

From windows in my father's house,
 Dreaming my dreams on winter nights,
I watched Orion as a girl
 Above another city's lights.

Years go, dreams go, and youth goes too,
 The world's heart breaks beneath its wars,
All things are changed, save in the east
 The faithful beauty of the stars.

From *Flame and Shadow*, 1920. Public domain.

On a projected slide, we annotate the focus of each stanza with notes like these:

1. The bloodshed of war is making me so sad

2. But then I look up at the stars which are constant, unchanged

3. And it brings back a memory of looking at those same stars as a child

4. Now I'm thinking about how almost everything changes over time, but other things never do

Another option, to help students make observations about logical ways to divide ideas, is to give them a poem that is only a few stanzas long but with the stanza breaks removed so that the poem looks like one long stanza. It is easy to do this on a PowerPoint slide or a half-page handout. The following list provides several poems that work well for this challenge, but as always, build your own lists and include poems that speak to you and your students.

Poems That Work Well for Stanza Study

1. "Keeping Quiet" by Robert Bly

2. "Those Winter Sundays" by Robert Hayden

3. "Democracy" by Langston Hughes

4. "Losing My Religion" by Ron Koertge

5. "New Yorkers" by Edward Field

6. "If Life Were Like Touch Football" by Julie Cadwallader Staub

Next, I tell students, "The word *stanza* comes to us from Latin and Italian and originally the word related to a room. So think of a poem as a house and a stanza a little room inside that house, a space where the poet has limited lines to explore part of a thought. The stanza breaks are like the walls. Here I have a house with all the walls removed. In its original form, this poem has [insert number of] stanzas. See if you can tell where the walls or stanza breaks should go."

After students have done this, I show them the original poem and they can check their stanza divisions alongside the original. "Now," I say, "let's talk about *why* these stanza breaks exist here. What shift occurs from the first to the second stanza? The second to the third? The third to the fourth?"

To transfer this ability to observe shifts within a text to our writing, we need to practice this more than once. "Our current writing project is going to be with us for a while. So over the next few days we are going to try this same technique with a few different poems, and by the end of the week, we'll even try it with a magazine article. When we draft our own essays, we are going to have to tune in to where those shifts happen. Even though we have an outline of where we are going in our writing, we don't *really* know how many paragraphs we have until we start writing. We can't. And unless they are working with a specific form of poetry with a specific number of stanzas, poets often figure this out as they go along and tweak it in revision too. It's what writers do. It's not easy work, but organizing your work with stanzas or paragraphs is a skill that you can develop."

This activity, practiced a few times, gives students the confidence to start breaking their work into "rooms" within ideas, to experiment with where to build the "walls" and form paragraphs in their papers. Writing about stanzas, poets Mark Strand and Eavan Boland remind us, "[The stanza] is as self-contained as any chamber or room. And yet to be in it is to have the consciousness at all times that it also leads somewhere" (cited in Larimer & Gannon, p. 87). This is the same consciousness we want our students to develop about paragraphing. What does this paragraph contain? Where does it move? Where do we pass through a door into the next room?

IT ALL COMES DOWN TO THIS

One of my ongoing struggles as I coach students through research writing is preventing our writing process from swallowing an entire marking period of instructional time. In research writing, students need to be incisive readers and discerning creators, simultaneously efficient, observant, and reflective. The balance of thinking fast and thinking slow is something we never perfectly achieve.

So if you read this chapter and think, "How would I ever pull off even one of these ideas without spinning my timeline for the unit—nay, for the year—completely out of control?!" you are not alone. As I read over this chapter, I reckon with the same thing!

Remember, the ideas shared here are acquired over years of practice coaching students through different research projects at different grade levels. I cannot think of a year when I used all of these ideas across a single unit, but if you do so successfully, I'd love to hear how you pulled it off!

Also remember that my students are conditioned to expect a Poem of the Day to start class each day, which makes any poetry sharing and writing a smooth, expected process.

Most of all, knowing your students and *what they need* will guide your selection and placement of poetry pauses no matter the genre. Selectiveness is especially important when working with research writing.

The following chart shows what strategies from this chapter I might use to meet specific needs in the course of our research project. I've tried to arrange them chronologically, but use your judgment and knowledge of your students as you choose which ones to apply and at what stage of the game.

Challenge Students Are Facing	Poetry Pause Strategy	Rationale
Students are reading a lot about their topic as they research but struggling to find the thread of connection between their sources and main points to develop.	A Found Poem	Found poems help students shine a light on the main points in their reading. They help find quotable passages within a text and identify the most important parts of a longer passage.

(Continued)

(Continued)

Challenge Students Are Facing	Poetry Pause Strategy	Rationale
Student drafts sound boring and clinical.	Poetry From Research	Having students work creatively for a little while can give them new eyes for their drafts and encourage the judicious use of strong word choice and figurative language in a research piece.
Student drafts lack structure or logical paragraphing.	Studying Stanza Breaks	Learning to think through stanza breaks gives some quick practical practice in noticing the shifts in focus that we need to tune into in order to paragraph our work in a way that makes it easy to understand. This strategy usually works best when we look at several poems over a period of time, identifying stanza breaks as we go.
Students need to synthesize information from a variety of sources to write about a process, procedure, or proposed solution to a problem.	How-To Poems	Writing one of these poems gives students the basic skeleton they need to see their process step-by-step, beginning to end. Additionally, strong action verbs tend to be central to this type of poem, so it sets students up for successful word choice in their essays.
Students are working on a multi-genre or multimodal research project that will not be presented in a traditional essay format.	Poetry From Research	This brief exercise in crossing genre boundaries helps prepare students to find what is engaging, entertaining, and aesthetically pleasing about their topic before they need to draft or design a finished product.

Most of all, integrating poetry pauses into the logical, organized process of a hefty research project prevents us from losing sight of the creative nature of *all* writing. This kind of creative and intellectual nimbleness prepares our students for life outside of school.

In *A Whole New Mind*, Daniel Pink's treatise on the fundamental importance of blending the best of our left-brain, logical thought with the best of our right-brain, emotional thought, he makes an intriguing observation: "Logic without emotion is a chilly, Spock-like existence. Emotion without logic is a weepy, hysterical world where the clocks are never right and the buses are always late. In the end, yin always needs yang." This is not just true socially, but cognitively too. He continues, "The two sides [of our brain] work in concert—two sections of an orchestra that sounds awful if one side packs up its instruments and goes home" (Pink, 2005, p. 25).

Likewise, writer Michael J. Gelb (1998) muses about Leonardo da Vinci's genius:

> Was Leonardo a scientist who studied art, or an artist who studied science? Clearly he was both. His scientific studies of rocks, plants, flight, flowing water, and human anatomy, for example, are expressed in beautiful, evocative, expressive works of art, not dry technical drawings. At the same time, the plans for his paintings and sculptures are exquisitely detailed, painstakingly analytical, and mathematically precise. (pp. 166-167)

Da Vinci's advice for painters was "Be sure you know the structure of all you wish to depict."

Bringing poetry to our research units orchestrates an approach that engages the whole mind, that pulls the best our brain has to offer, logically and creatively, bringing kaleidoscopic possibilities to what is often the capstone project of an entire course.

6

POETRY PAUSES FOR IMPROVING GRAMMAR AND PUNCTUATION SKILLS

If you have taught secondary English for even a few years, you have probably had an experience like this: The chemistry teacher comes to you groaning, "Why don't these kids know how to write? I can barely read their papers. Their *grammar* is so *bad*!"

There is a terrible shrinking feeling an English teacher gets when confronted with that question. We want our students to transfer their grammatical and mechanical skills to every academic setting, but too often, they do not.

Linda Bergmann and Janet Zepernick (2007) studied this phenomenon with a focus group of confident college student writers. The researchers were curious to learn about how students perceive their own writing process and how teachers can improve the transfer of writing skills from English classes to other academic disciplines.

The college students in this study "commonly mentioned revision as one of the 'secrets' of good writing, although they talked primarily about avoiding it. One student said: 'I do find myself at times restructuring my sentences. I personally hate to admit that I did something wrong. But occasionally I will look at something I've written and say "well, that's extra and that's extra and I can take it out," and I will modify it, so I guess I didn't get it quite right at first'" (Bergmann & Zepernick, 2007, pp.136-137). This student still believes that "getting it right at first" is better than "doing something wrong" in one's writing and revising it.

Another student said, "'I've been told many, many times that the secret to good writing is rewriting. I agree that that's a good secret, but I'm not patient enough for it to help me, and I just don't like it.' Although students generally identified revision as an important tool for competent writers, in actual practice, revision contributed little to their own writing competence" (Bergmann & Zepernick, 2007, p. 137).

Additionally, the study found that these students perceived grammar skills as essential only for English courses and primarily about error avoidance rather than craftsmanship.

Likely, as a reader of this book, you already teach grammar in the context of writing and know that revision is the key step of the writing process where we can manipulate the grammar of a text to achieve the best effect for our audience. You are not like the college professors mentioned by some of the students who "only circled the commas" and considered it grammar instruction. But the interviews in this study make an important point: student writers who eschewed revision also had an error/deficit view of grammar. To them, grammar is about rules and repair, not style and construction. It is about fixing the leaky roof, not adding a turret or a solar panel.

Two things are likely true in your own observation in working with students that also bubbled up in this research study:

1. Students sometimes fail to see how the creative and technical aspects of writing enhance each other.
2. Students do not always value grammar skills in a way that helps them communicate well across content areas and beyond graded assessments.

Because poetry builds bridges between creative expression and the logical development of ideas, it is poised to help students bridge the gap between grammar as a creative device and grammar as a technical skill, uniting creativity and correctness.

Here are a few reasons poetry can work well to help students harness the power of grammatical structures, punctuation, and mechanics in language:

1. **Since poems are short, students can see the impact of revisions in their poetry more quickly than they do in their essays**

and papers. It is kind of like the difference between redesigning a corner of a room versus redesigning your entire house. The corner redesign feels fulfilling after just a little while; the whole house project has a pay-off, but only after an extended commitment.

2. **Because many poems are crafted around patterns and repetition, readers notice grammatical structures more than once in a short space.** This provides organic practice as we closely read and then imitate a poem.

3. **Punctuation in poems is abundant and playful.** Many poets model conventional usage of a punctuation mark that students can immediately transfer to their writing. Other poets defy the rules, and these too can make for valuable conversations about how and why they differ from conventional usage.

4. **Line breaks often assist readers in parsing the grammar of a poem.** Breaking longer sentences into smaller parts can help students to see the structures that hold our language together more clearly. Even enjambment, which messes with our perceptions a bit, can lead to good discussion about parts of speech and grammatical structure within a sentence *because* it interrupts our grammatical expectations.

Since this book emphasizes the practical ideas we can use in our classroom, let's look at some of the grammatical skills we hope our students learn to employ, and dare I say enjoy, during a productive revision process. Many of these structures can transfer across genres, and your teaching will be the most powerful if you can demonstrate how these structures found in poetry can improve clarity in a lab report or breathe life into an analysis piece for AP European History class.

POETRY PAUSE: PARSING WITH LINE BREAKS

Poem: A line from *Nature Stories* by Jules Renard

Plan: Introduce a line of figurative language as a one-line poem. Invite students to split the poem up into more than one line with line breaks.

Big Picture: Sometimes students struggle to see the grammatical parts of the whole. When we invite them to break a sentence into poetic lines, these parts become clearer.

One day, for Poem of the Day, I surprise my students with this line from Jules Renard (2010) and tell them it's a one-line poem (see Figure 6.1). This stretches the truth a bit. It is actually one sentence from an illustrated children's book.

6.1. **An excerpt from Jules Renard.**

THIS LOVE-LETTER FOLDED IN TWO IS LOOKING FOR A FLOWER'S ADDRESS.

BY JULES RENARD

From *Nature Stories* by Jules Renard, translated by Douglas Parmée, ©2010

I tell students to copy it from the screen into their notebooks while splitting it into more than one line. "Two is plenty, but if you want to split it into more than two lines, go for it. Where does it feel like a line break would make this into more of a traditional short poem?"

After two minutes pass, I say, "OK, now I'd like to make a prediction." I pull out my digital pen with great gravitas so I can mark up a projected image of the poem. "How many of you made line break here, right after the word 'two.'" Many hands go up. "And if you did three or four lines, I'm willing to bet that the breaks are after 'love-letter' and 'looking.' Am I right?" In most cases I am.

"Can I show you how I made that prediction?"

I have baited the hook for a quick look into grammar. Subject and predicate, noun phrases, adjective phrases, and prepositional phrases are boring in a vacuum, but when these concepts explain the English teacher's psychic ability to predict writer's notebook results, they become more palatable.

I explain that my predictions were possible because language, even when it is as short as a simple sentence, breaks down into smaller parts, much like molecules break down into atoms. When we are forced to break down the sentence, as we just did in our line break challenge, it snaps apart in those logical places.

"There's a verb for what we just did here when we made these line breaks: parse," I tell them. "When you take a piece of language and deconstruct it, analyze its parts, you 'parse' it. Part of the reason grammar can be so hard to learn in a language we already read is that we are slowing down a process that happens quickly when we read. Our brains automatically smooth the joints between parts of a sentence. But we also need to break language apart if we aim to improve our writing. It's worth it. Let me show you why."

With just one metaphorical line about a butterfly, they are hooked and ready for more.

I do not insist on students remembering the parts I named in that sentence. I do want them to remember that parsing sentences is something that will help them understand how the sentences work and how to build even better ones.

POETRY PAUSE: POETIC PARALLEL LINES

> **Poem:** an excerpt from "Love" by Alex Dimitrov
>
> **Plan:** After defining *anaphora* with a pop-culture example, students examine how it works in a poem with a goal of applying it to another piece of writing.
>
> **Big Picture:** Anaphora, or parallel structure, is one way writers build momentum with their words. This establishes rhythm in a poem, but it also works well as an argument gathers steam or as an emotion heightens in a narrative. It is a highly transferable skill that is engaging to teach and fun to use.

Whether you prefer to call the purposeful repetition of grammatical lines by its Greek term, *anaphora*, or it's more modern name, *parallelism*, is up to you. I tend to use parallelism because it creates an instant point of reference from math class. I ask students, "What do you know about parallel lines? Let's draw three in our notebook. What do parallel lines that we draw *do* on the page?"

From their math teachers, they know this: "They run the same direction, near each other, but without touching."

I draw three parallel lines on the board and say, "Good! Let's look at how writers can do this with language. The same kind of thing happens all the time in poems, in songs and speeches, in the articles you read online, but you may have never noticed it before. Once you do, and you learn how to create parallel lines in your writing, you learn how to gather momentum in a piece, like a wave rolling in from the sea or storm clouds gathering in the sky. Learning to write parallel lines gives you power!"

Julius Caesar's famous line, "I came, I saw, I conquered!" is an excellent place to start since the parallel structure is so simple. Pronoun + verb, pronoun + verb, pronoun + verb—voila! A memorable line that has endured for centuries. In her article for the Poetry Foundation, Rebecca Hazelton (2013) uses other famous speeches to exemplify this tactic, from portions of Martin Luther King's "I Have a Dream," to Winston Churchill's 1940 speech before the Commons, to an impassioned speech by Homer Simpson in the 1994 episode "Fear of Flying." This technique abounds in commercials—just tune your ear to the parallel lines next time you are interrupted on Hulu to hear about a product for thirty seconds.

Scan this QR code to watch a ten-minute speech from Elie Wiesel with abundant examples of anaphora.

Alex Dimitrov's poem "Love" is many pages long, but within the first twelve lines, the anaphora is clear:

I love you early in the morning and it is difficult to love you.

I love the January sky and knowing it will change although unlike us.

I love watching people read.

I love photo booths.

I love midnight.

I love writing letters and this is my letter. To the world that never wrote to me.

I love snow and briefly.

I love the first minutes in a warm room after stepping out of the cold.

I love my twenties and want them back every day.

I love time.

I love people.

I love people and my time away from them the most.

Excerpted from "Love" by Alex Dimitrov, *American Poetry Review*, Vol. 49, No.1 (2020).

PRO TIP

If you need more scaffolding to introduce or review anaphora, try using a children's poem, like the picture book *I Am Enough* by Grace Byers, using Scaffolding Strategy 4 in Appendix A.

The poem shrinks and swells, moving from those tiny "first minutes in a warm room" to the enormity of "time" and the generality of "people." I love that. But it also maintains the metronome of those two opening words: "I love." These parallel lines cradle us with their rhythm.

To introduce the idea of parallel lines in our writing, I invite students to continue this poem with the same start to each line but using some of their own ideas. What do they love?

Here's what Billy created:

> I love fishing, the waiting.
> I love car rides.
> I love my family, the fights.
> I love my cousins, especially the boxing.
> I love the summer evenings sitting by the bay.

Brooke picked up on Dimitrov's pattern of lines that swell out from an initially simple idea:

> I love the breeze
> I love the cold winter
> I love the snow-covered homes
> I love the fireplaces, burning alive.
> I love the warmth
> I love the cocoa
> I love the blankets
> I love the people there enjoying it.

Sometime later in the course, while working on an essay, article, or narrative, challenge students to write a poem about their topic: eight to twelve lines long with the same two or three words at the start of each line. After reading their poem aloud with a partner, hearing their own words, have students choose three or four of those sentences that they could incorporate into their paragraphs as they revise.

I might say, "Where do you need a soundtrack in this piece? An emotional tug or forceful crescendo? Parallel lines can help you with this. Watch how the impact of your words heightens when you pull a few of your best sentences out of a poem and into paragraph."

Jessica wrote these lines of anaphora poetry about Art Spiegelman's reasons for writing *Maus*.

He writes to share
He writes to let others know
He writes because it's important
He writes because it caused pain
He writes because to forget is a crime
He writes because it is memory
He writes because it matters
He writes because he wants to get closer to his dad

After creating this writer's notebook poem in about three minutes, I asked Jessica to pick her three best sentences to arrange into parallel lines in a paragraph about the author's purpose. Here is what she did:

"Art Spiegelman writes because to forget is a crime. He writes because it keeps memories. He writes because he wants to get closer to his dad."

These lines create momentum in a paragraph just as well as they do in a poem, and by asking Jessica to overwrite a bit at first, to create more lines than she needed to include in her essay, she paused with a poem to pay attention to the interplay of ideas and words in her writing. And she ended up with a powerful, useful parallel structure.

Poems to Demonstrate Parallel Structure

1. "Remember" by Joy Harjo

2. "Daily" by Naomi Shihab Nye

3. "The Delight Song of Tsoai-talee" by N. Scott Momaday

4. Excerpts from "Song of Myself" by Walt Whitman

5. "Tell Me Again How You Don't See Color" by Marshall Gillson

6. "At the Spring Dawn" by Angelina Weld Grimké

POETRY PAUSE: "POETRY IS ALL NOUNS AND VERBS"

Poem: "Getting It Right" by Kevin Carey

Plan: Inventory the nouns and verbs in a poem to demonstrate how precision and clarity with these two parts of speech can be the bones of a piece of writing.

Big Picture: Student writers understand at an early age that word choice matters, but they sometimes acquire the habit of slathering on more adjectives, thinking this improves their writing. This lesson helps them briefly examine the power of nouns and verbs in a poem and then immediately transfer those observations to their own drafts to simplify or strengthen their writing.

This subheading title, "Poetry Is All Nouns and Verbs," is a quote from poet Marianne Moore that I have shared with my students every year. In identifying poetry as "all nouns and verbs," Moore boils the genre down to its essence in a phrase that is as much an earworm as it is a truth.

But the great thing about this quote is that it does not just apply to poetry. Good writing is all about the nouns and verbs, the bones we use to build meaning. Someone or something (noun) does something (verb). There is an act of creation in this form, a simple elegance.

Verlyn Klinkenborg's book *Several Short Sentences About Writing* (2012) recommends "unlearning" the traditional lessons about writing with their emphasis on transitions and the perception that longer is better. Rather, he says, "Writing short sentences will help you write strong, balanced sentences of any length. Strong, lengthy sentences are really just strong, short sentences joined in various ways" (p. 10). He invites his readers to "imagine it this way: One by one, each sentence takes the stage. It says the very thing it comes into existence to say. Then it leaves the stage" (p. 3).

He crafts his book with the same, simple clarity that he praises, expressing each thought with precise nouns and verbs. Each page looks a bit like a poem with line breaks and white space partitioning ideas and without the traditional indentation and paragraphing we associate with prose.

A poem that can help our students begin to see the simple, elegant power of sentences built from strong nouns and verbs is "Getting It Right" by Kevin Carey. It's a beautiful memoir poem that's easy to understand on a first read and only gets better with repeated read-ings. The choice of nouns and verbs is part of what makes it so.

GETTING IT RIGHT

by Kevin Carey

In grammar school I stuttered,
felt the hot panic on my face
when my turn to read crept up the row.

Even when I counted the paragraphs
and memorized the passage,
I'd trip on the first or second word,

and then it would be over,
the awful hesitation, the word
clinging to the lining of my throat

rising only too late to avoid
the laughter around me. I was never
the smartest kid in the room,

but I had answers I knew were right
yet was afraid to say them.
Years later, it all came out, flowing

sentences I practiced over and over,
Shakespeare or Frost, my own tall tales
in low-lit barrooms, scribbled

in black-bound journals, rehearsing,
anticipating my turn, my time,
a way of finally getting it right.

"Getting it Right" by Kevin Carey, The Writer's Almanac with Garrison Keillor, 2016.

Of course, on the first read we have to just admire the story and idea in this poem for a second, talk about things in our lives that might feel like this, triumphs earned through time and practice. There is hard-scrabble hope in this poem that we can all relate to.

But then I say, "Let's list every verb in this poem. Just start calling them out. What are all the actions here?" I might circle these on a PowerPoint slide or start a list on the whiteboard, depending on the setting. These words start to populate our list: stuttered, felt, crept, memorized, counted, trip, clinging, rising, practiced, scribbled, rehearsing, anticipating.

"What are the effects of these verbs? What patterns do you see?" Students notice how they move from past to present when we arrange them chronologically, from hesitation to confidence. Without even knowing what the whole poem is about, just seeing this list of verbs would clue us in to the arc of this story and the shift in mood.

PRO TIP

If you need to scaffold this activity a bit more, the "Think, Pair, Share" Scaffolding Strategy 3 in Appendix A works especially well with this poem.

"Now, where are the nouns? The things the poet wants us to look at or abstract emotions he wants us to feel along with him? Call them out!"

We circle words like *school, panic, row, paragraph, passage, hesitation, throat, laughter, room, sentences, barrooms, journals, time.* "What do you notice about this set of nouns?" Student might point out that several establish settings, and many relate to words or to school.

The beauty of this poem is its simplicity, which allows us to make these observations and quickly get down to our larger writing projects. I elaborate: "So what can we take from this? What's the big idea? Simple language has power. And specific nouns and specific verbs have a special power. If we put them together, we can show our reader just about anything. And there is a huge difference between reading this poem and reading the sentence that says, 'I used to stutter in school, but with practice I overcame it,' even though they communicate the same central idea. Why is the poem more memorable and vivid? There are more nouns and verbs. The writer zooms in and shows us what to notice. This can make any piece of writing stronger."

Immediately moving from this poetry pause to a paragraph in their drafts and underlining every noun and verb they find can be a valuable interrogation. Which of these words are already specific? Where can we move the reader to look more closely at the parts of a big picture? Where are the "action verb deserts" in our work, the places where we rely on linking verbs like "was" or "seemed" or "felt" that leave the reader with nothing specific to visualize? The more action verbs we can incorporate in our writing, even argument or research writing, the more vivid the writing becomes.

Sometimes after this lesson I even provide lists of strong action verbs. For a narrative piece, there are verb lists aplenty online, but Figure 6.2 provides an example of an illustrated verb list I put together to help my students craft an analysis piece that still employs strong action verbs.

6.2. An illustrated anchor chart of strong verbs to improve essays.

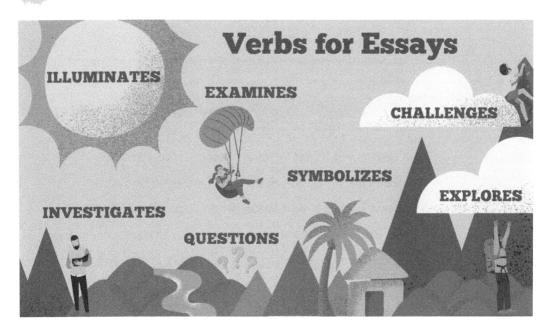

Our students can write with much more authority when they say an author "examines," "investigates," or "illuminates" an idea in their writing rather than simply stating what the author "writes," "says," or even worse, "is trying to say." Creating a list or anchor chart of strong action verbs that work for your students in a particular assignment builds a bridge between their observations about the power of verbs in a poem and their usage of strong verbs in an essay.

Many poems provide evidence that simple, specific nouns and verbs have a special power. I have listed a few of these poems in the following box. After reading them, you may even challenge your students to find a home for one of the verbs in the poem in their own writing. We have lots of underused verbs in our vocabulary attics. We know what the words mean, but we may not be apt to use them in our first drafts. Revision lets us dust them off, bring them down, and redesign a corner of our room.

Poems to Draw Our Attention to Nouns and Verbs

1. "Child on Top of a Greenhouse" by Theodore Roethke - memoir writing

2. "dog" by Valerie Worth - descriptive writing

3. "Wyoming Highways" by William Notter - technical writing

4. "Makin' Jump Shots" by Robert Harper - sports writing

5. "Shoulders" by Naomi Shihab Nye - narrative scene writing

6. "Daisy" by Amy Ludwig VanDerwater - character development

7. "We Never Know" by Yusef Komunyakaa - narrative scene writing

8. "The Playground Elegy" by Clint Smith - argument writing

9. "When the Virus Comes" by Angelo Geter - analysis writing

10. "Beethoven" by Shane Koyczan - research writing

POETRY PAUSE: PREPOSITION POEMS

Poems: "Where Do Poems Come From" by Leo and "Where Did My CheezIt Go?" by Remy

Plan: Using a list of prepositions and a list of suggested titles, students create a silly poem that practices using a plethora of prepositions.

Big Picture: Teachers who defend worksheets as learning tools for grammar skills often feel that this is the only way to help students see a structure or pattern with enough repetition and practice to move toward mastery. Poetry often offers built-in repetition, and asking our students to write poems that employ a given grammatical technique gives them practice that is both repetitive and creative.

One of the earliest types of phrases students learn about and practice using is the prepositional phrase, which specifies the place or timing of something they write about.

Through the years, teachers have come up with all sorts of mnemonic devices to help students remember prepositions. Maybe you are familiar with one of the preposition songs on YouTube or the airplane/cloud sketch many teachers use: "The airplane can be *above* the cloud, *under* the cloud, *in* the cloud, moving *through* the cloud."

These techniques can be useful in memorizing a list of prepositions and even their purpose, but writing a preposition poem gives students quick hands-on practice actually *using* this valuable set of words in their writer's notebooks. So after introducing and reviewing what a preposition is and how it functions, often using the plane-and-cloud method, I bring a brief poetry writing exercise to my students that begins with the visual in Figure 6.3.

6.3. Preposition Poems visual

"Here is a list of titles to choose from," I say, "but of course you can create a different title if you come up with one that interests you more. Use some of the prepositions in the list on the right to craft a poem out of a series of prepositional phrases. You can lay this out on a page however you would like, but for this first draft, I want it to be just a series of prepositional phrases."

Here are some examples of what middle school students created with this quick prompt. This one is from seventh grader Leo, who started with a list in his notebook, then rearranged the list into this poem to achieve a better sound:

WHERE DO DREAMS COME FROM?

within the mind,
below consciousness,
beneath our thoughts,
beyond reality,
amid imagination,
among the cherished

And the poems do not have to be deep and ponderous to allow for plenty of prepositional practice. Remy, a sixth grader, chose a more whimsical direction:

WHERE DID MY CHEEZIT GO?

across the yard
beyond the street
over the roof
under the dirt
through the ground
and there it stays

An assignment like this one can be adapted to all sorts of grammatical structures. A poem can be a series of simple sentences, dependent clauses, or participial phrases.

Our students will find a study of a grammatical structures impactful only if they can apply what they learn in their writing. This functions with the same repeated practice as a worksheet, but it feels far more fun.

PRO TIP

If a student needs some instructional intervention about a type of phrase, try creating a few fill-in-the-blank frames, using Scaffolding Strategy 2 from Appendix A.

Any need for clarification becomes apparent as you walk through the classroom and glance at writers' notebooks. Your error-spotting is a means of formative assessment, guiding your next steps rather than red-penned point deductions. Moreover, this method helps our students learn by *doing*, by *creating* something on a blank page. This makes them more likely to retain the concept and appreciate its value to writers.

POETRY PAUSE: DIALOGUE RULES

Poems: "A Man Said to the Universe" by Stephen Crane and "After Forty Years of Marriage She Tries a New Recipe for Hamburger Hot Dish" by Leo Dangel

Plan: Share a short poem that models the conventions of dialogue and annotate the details of those conventions together as a class.

Big Picture: Dialogue conventions can be pesky when students draft narratives, but poems give us a tinier text in which to point out and discuss the details students can apply to their drafts. Moreover, we can study the features of a dialogue quickly in a poetry pause and then move into editing work in a longer piece of writing, so that the transfer of this skill happens immediately in the classroom, the same day as our instruction.

We often teach the conventions of crafting dialogue as parts of our narrative units. Students have been looking at models of dialogue in the books they read for over a decade by the time they reach my class. I am always surprised how few of them seem to internalize the details—a new paragraph for each new speaker, capitalization patterns, periods and commas within the quotation marks—by the time they reach high school.

I always encourage students to go back and find a scene from a favorite book lurking untouched on their bookshelf. I tell them to slow down and notice how the author applies the rules to create an effect that has stuck with them over time.

Some poems provide examples of dialogue conventions as well. An especially brief example is Stephen Crane's "A Man Said to the Universe."

A MAN SAID TO THE UNIVERSE

by Stephen Crane

A man said to the universe:
"Sir, I exist!"
"However," replied the universe,
"The fact has not created in me
A sense of obligation."

From *War is Kind*, 1899. Public domain.

This poem is so short that I might hand out tiny paper copies for students to tape in their notebooks to annotate, or even ask them to copy it from the projector screen. The meaning of this poem does not take long to explore: Crane basically states the universe does not feel it owes us anything, and our existence is so, so small in the grand scheme of things. But I do not really dwell on this. Instead, we look at and annotate some of the dialogue rules the author applies.

With your students, observe the capitalization and punctuation in this piece. Why are the exclamation point, comma, and period inside the quotation marks while the colon is not? Why are "Sir," "However," and "The" capitalized, but "replied" is not? Where are the endmarks in relation to the quotation marks?

Try rewriting the poem in prose. Do any of these details change? If so, why?

Leo Dangel's hilarious poem "After Forty Years of Marriage, She Tries a New Recipe for Hamburger Hot Dish" is another excellent vehicle for discussing dialogue conventions such as paragraphing and tag lines, though first your students will love discussing the two perspectives in this simmering domestic dispute.

AFTER FORTY YEARS OF MARRIAGE, SHE TRIES A NEW RECIPE FOR HAMBURGER HOT DISH

by Leo Dangel

"How did you like it?" she asked.

"It's all right," he said.

"This is the third time I cooked
it this way. Why can't you
ever say if you like something?"

"Well if I didn't like it, I
wouldn't eat it," he said.

"You never can say anything
I cook tastes good."

"I don't know why all the time
you think I have to say it's good.
I eat it, don't I?"

"I don't think you have to say
all the time it's good, but once
in awhile you could say
you like it."

"It's all right," he said.

"After Forty Years of Marriage She Tries a New Recipe For Hamburger Hot Dish" by Leo Dangel, from *Old Man Brunner Country*, Spoon River Poetry Press, 1987.

"Who is right here?" I ask first. "Is this guy being a jerk? Or is this wife too demanding?" If you are looking for proof your students have learned something from your class about using textual evidence, that question will open the floodgates, and you are sure to laugh together!

But then I add, "There is something else we really need to zero in on here. Look at a few of the dialogue rules this poet follows to help make clear who is speaking at any point in the poem. These are rules you will need to follow to add clarity to your narratives as well!"

Together we notice:

- Each time the speaker changes, we get a new stanza. This is the same thing that happens with paragraphing in prose writing. A new speaker gets a new paragraph. As I like to put it, the person who speaks "owns" the paragraph, and when someone new speaks, they get their own new paragraph.

- The tag lines that identify the speaker, like "he said," are attached with commas that come inside the quotation marks.

- The tag lines begin with lowercase letters, even when they follow a full stop, as in the first one, "she asked" which follows a question mark. I explain, "Even though these contain a subject and a verb, these are not complete sentences that can stand on their own. They are called 'tag lines' because all they do is tag the speaker, and they are considered an extended part of the spoken sentence."

In my experience, no matter how many times I have students look at a mentor text from their favorite book, they overlook these details unless we explicitly review them. So while mentorship from prose is critical, breaking down the piece, identifying the patterns, and explaining the rules with a poem that applies the rules for dialogue tends to result in better transfer when editing their own work. Students have the chance to work as a class with a particular rule in the microcosm of a poem before applying it back to the larger landscape of their own creative piece.

POETRY PAUSE: EXAMINING RARE PUNCTUATION SPECIES

Poems: Various, depending on the punctuation mark. See the table below.

Plan: Share a poem with the aim of examining the effect a mark of punctuation has on the text.

Big Picture: When we help students learn to use the broader array of punctuation marks in our language, we demonstrate how to add shades of meaning to their writing. We can choose some poems where the meaning is not our central focus, but the nuts and bolts that hold it together (e.g., semicolons, dashes, ellipses) become models for our students.

Commas are the pigeons of the punctuation world. They are ubiquitous. Pigeons are beautiful when you pause to really look at them—their courage, their iridescence. And like commas, when pigeons are in the wrong place at the wrong time, they can be annoying. (My wife nearly did not marry me after I teased her about a comma splice in her e-mail during our engagement!)

Some teachers seem to believe that punctuation instruction should focus primarily on commas because they are so common and erroneous commas can be so glaring. A colleague who teaches science at my school recently told me about a high school teacher who drilled his students in twelve comma rules, and he still remembers them.

This obsession is understandable, but at the same time, it can torpedo our efforts to help students truly experience the joy—there, I said it—the *joy* in punctuation. After all, who could learn to enjoy birdwatching if the prerequisite to finding woodpeckers and eagles and scarlet tanagers was a comprehensive understanding of pigeons?

It is OK, even important, to move our students forward in examining the rarer species of punctuation before they have mastered the comma. They can keep learning about pigeons and eagles at the same time.

Punctuation shapes meaning in the texts our students create just as much as the words they choose. Students are often surprised to learn that punctuation was not a part of the earliest written forms of English; the practice emerged a few hundred years ago to add clarity. Contrary to what students believe, punctuation simplified the language rather than complicated it, and the specific usage rules emerged over time. Sometimes poetry has even helped develop these rules. An "On Poetry" column in *The New York Times* went so far as to give this phenomenon two different metaphors in its headline: "How Poets Use Punctuation as a Superpower and a Secret Weapon" (Gabbert, 2020). Poets are particularly brave in exploring the use of punctuation and the way it can shape meaning.

In my Poem of the Day slideshow, I keep a section labeled "Punctuation Poems" to help me keep track of verses that are particularly good for exemplifying the power of punctuation marks. In the following table, I share a few of my favorites and some notes about how I introduce the punctuation mark in my classroom. As you integrate more poetry, you will find more poems to add to your list, and I encourage you to use the white space in this table to jot down a few as you come across them . . . or start your own slideshow file and watch it grow!

Studying punctuation in the context of poetry provides quick practice and playful experimentation that is sometimes lost in our study of the mechanics of language. Poetry pauses can help students see punctuation as a choice that achieves an effect rather than a list of rules to memorize and apply.

Scan this QR code to access the table pictured below with links to all of the poems.

Punctuation Mark	Poem(s)	Notes
hyphen	"The Red Wing Church" by Ted Kooser	After learning about how hyphens work, I share an image of Ted Kooser's poem with the hyphens removed and tell students I took out three hyphens from the poem. Can they tell where they used to be? Then we discuss why the words *tar-paper*, *glassed-in*, and *stained-glass* are hyphenated in this poem.
	"The Dream Keeper" by Langston Hughes	Hughes's poem demonstrates in a short space how the hyphen can be used to create a new noun (*cloud-cloth*) and a new adjective (*too-rough*).

(Continued)

Punctuation Mark	Poem(s)	Notes
dash	"Fueled" by Marci Hans	I often like to share that one way to use an em dash is as "a comma with more drama," and Hans's poem is the perfect example, adding gravitas by replacing every comma with a dash.
	"My life had stood - a loaded gun" by Emily Dickinson	Dickinson's poem may work best for an advanced class of students, because the meaning of the poem is not particularly clear on the first read. But this poet is known for her unusual use of the dash, and we might use this or another one of her poems to look at where she is using the dash as a rule follower and where she is breaking the rules to use a dash.
ellipsis	"The Green Canoe" by Jeffrey Harrison	This is a poem that is about literally drifting in a canoe, so when the first stanza ends in an ellipsis, it's a perfect time to talk about the drifting, trailing-off effect of this punctuation mark.
parentheses	"How Will the Pandemic Affect Poetry?" by Julia Alvarez	The third line of this poem breaks individual words apart from each other, replicating the way humans had to mask and social distance during the COVID-19 pandemic. Students love discussing why she chose parentheses to create this effect and what meaning the punctuation adds to the line.
	"(citizen) (illegal)" by Jose Olivarez	This poem has an unusual use of parentheses that will be fascinating to discuss with your students. What purpose does this punctuation serve in this context, and how does that relate to the way parentheses are normally used?
semicolon	"Twilight Field" by Gabriel Fried	This delightfully creepy four-line poem has only one semicolon, but it is a perfect example of how this punctuation works. It follows with a few short sentences, which makes for an interesting discussion: Why does the poet choose to use a semicolon to connect the first two sentences but leave the other short sentences separated by periods?

Punctuation Mark	Poem(s)	Notes
colon	"About Competition" by Charles Bukowski	Bukowski's poem gives an excellent example of a colon introducing a big reveal at the end of a sentence. I tell my students, "Colons are like firecrackers. What comes before a colon is the ascent, then the colon is the pop, and what comes after is the big deal, the sizzling, falling light everyone comes to see. Colons create that same effect, highlighting what comes after."
	"Barrier Island" by Floyd Skloot	Skloot's poem about an abandoned carnival space is easy to understand on a first read, and it presents a great blended approach to using a colon. It uses a colon to connect a list of images to an independent clause, but in this poem, the series comes before the clause. This allows the poet to double-dip a little bit, using the firecracker reveal effect mentioned above.
colon and commas in a series	"Swift Things Are Beautiful" by Elizabeth Coatsworth	Coatsworth's poem provides an excellent example of how an independent clause and a colon can introduce a series and then how commas can keep that series going. We often write a poem together in small groups or as a class using two different contrasts, perhaps "tall" and "short" or "large" and "small," following the same punctuation pattern as the original.

IT ALL COMES DOWN TO THIS

I do not think that everything our students need to know about the way our language works can be taught well through poems.

Instead, these techniques aspire to help students see revision of their work as something more than teacher-pleasing and instead as an empowering, creative act. Engage in these activities with them, in your notebook or on the whiteboard or under the document camera. If you let students see *your* revision, *your* playfulness, and the way the poems inspire *you* to redesign your words for a better effect, the greater the chance they too will become excited at the prospect of revising their work.

Throughout this book, I've made numerous allusions to the fact that I write with my students. When it comes to teaching the grammar, conventions, mechanics, the nitty-gritty details of how our language works and how we can best apply its tools, writing with students becomes even more crucial.

A study of pre-service teachers revealed that out of 192 teachers interviewed, 109 considered themselves poor writers. Think about that for a minute. Many teachers who aspire to help students grow as writers lack confidence in themselves as writers! Cassandra Sacher (2016) observes about this study, "Indeed, some teachers feel so unconfident in their teaching of writing that they neglect to change their instruction despite the evidence proving it to be ineffective. One example of this is the preponderance of grammar instruction that abounds in high school classrooms across the country masquerading as writing instruction" (p. 49).

Yes, substituting direct instruction in grammar for quality, embedded instruction in how language impacts our writing may have more to do with teachers' own insecurities as writers than it does with their experience, research, or skill. Worksheets and answer keys are simpler than thinking through the decisions writers make, for the student and the teacher. This does not mean worksheets are better.

As we craft poems with parallel structure inspired by mentor texts, as we let our students see our drafts evolve through better verbs, streamlined syntax, and more effective punctuation, let's make it our resolve to embrace the messiness and the insecurities writing brings into our lives. These same feelings encroach on our students as they write too. Let's show them it's OK to wrestle with language a bit, and things end up sounding better when we do.

Prolific writer James Michener, who grew up in the Pennsylvania town where I teach, once famously said, "I'm not a very good writer, but I'm an excellent rewriter." I have this quote hanging in the wall of my classroom to remind my students—and myself, if I am being entirely honest here—that revision really is where the magic happens. Our students should know that revision is not just an expectation for them but that their teacher, the most experienced writer in the room, also knows the power of putting in the elbow grease, bending and polishing language.

POETRY AS A HEALTHY LITERACY ROUTINE

The more I catch up with friends, family, and acquaintances and hear about their experiences during the past several turbulent years, the more I realize that everyone has changed. Collectively and individually, we reckoned with loss, disruption, and widening divisions. Working in schools, we witnessed board meetings erupt in unprecedented theatrics, we helped students through struggles with anxiety and depression, we reckoned with inequities in our educational systems, and we lifted our shields against the increasing vilification of teachers and books.

Despite all of this frustration, almost everyone mentions a silver lining or two. During these same years we had the rare opportunity to pause, regroup, and take an account of our priorities as shutdowns, quarantines, and common sense made everyone spend more time at home for a while. And even though the world was "too much with us" as we doomscrolled and fretted about the herky-jerky return to some sort of normality, the pandemic gave us a pause from the "getting and spending" that William Wordsworth once wrote about, the mad rush that generally defines our twenty-first-century existence. There were valuable discoveries in those pauses.

Poetry pauses offer us the gift of discovery. They invite us to slow down and think. They invite us to craft our thinking alongside some of the most inventive, technically talented writers to have ever lived. Poetry can offer a salve, a poke, a hug, a challenge, an inscrutable mystery or an immutable truth. We just need to slow down enough to notice.

If there is one broad stroke to remember from this book as you apply it to your classroom, it is the power of close observation that poetry offers. D. H. Lawrence once said, "Poetry is an act of attention." Poet Gregory Welch (2020) expands on this: "Poetry is a bit like lacing a pair of shoes. You have to wind things together, pull them tight, tie a knot or two and combine things that might feel impossible the first few times but could eventually come together in a stronger whole" (para. 16). "The real secret ingredient to all of this is being observant" (para. 20). Attention to detail is an endangered but teachable skill, one that we hope our students transfer to all sorts of other aspects of their lives beyond English class.

This concluding chapter will look at how teachers can build their own poetry exposure over time, help students to keep up the habit outside of class, and even share an idea that helps students revisit the feedback we give them in their writing. In short, we will pause and digest how we can make the ideas in this book work fluently in our classrooms and open space for our own growth with these ideas over time.

BUILDING THE CLASSROOM LIBRARY

Building a classroom library and keeping books to share with students at our fingertips is not a new idea. Most English teachers I know are constantly building, curating, and weeding a library in their own classroom to maintain a collection of books that meets the needs of their students. As the students in front of them change, so change the needs, so changes the collection.

Every classroom library deserves a poetry section. I would like to make a few suggestions about specific books and sources of ongoing recommendations of what to put there so that this shelf can be diverse and meet the needs of your students. Here are a few ideas to get you started with the anthologies and collections that are best for your students:

- More and more collections are being developed for young readers. The *Poetry Speak: Who I Am* anthology brings diverse voices together to show teens how poems can express identity while *The Poetry Remedy* anthology "prescribes" just-right poems for a plethora of reader moods.

- Scholastic publishes a collection of classic, canonical poems from Kipling, Coleridge, Poe, and others in illustrated, kid-friendly picture book form called *Poetry for Young People*.

- Billy Collins has gathered his *Poetry 180* and *180 More* anthologies to help promote spoken readings of poetry every day in high school classrooms, and the Library of Congress maintains an updated online collection of these on their website.

- Button Poetry has its own publishing house, allowing you to collect books written by the spoken word poets our students meet on YouTube. The #teachlivingpoets crowd will provide high school teachers with an ongoing stream of new poetry collection recommendations that speak to the present moment, appeal to high school students, and spotlight BIPOC poets.

- Kwame Alexander, Irene Latham and Charles Waters, and Georgia Heard have edited anthologies for young people, and the many, many anthologies by Lee Bennet Hopkins speak to students of all ages, not just the elementary students for whom they are designed.

- Janet Wong and Sylvia Vardell's publishing company, Pomelo Books, has a catalogue full of children's poetry anthologies: one for administrators looking to share a poem over the loudspeaker each day, one for teachers looking to incorporate movement into their lessons, and one to integrate poetry with science class. Their creative anthologizing is boundless, and this is a publisher to watch, especially if you work with younger middle school students.

PRO TIP

Social media can yield a vast array of poems and poetry book recommendations. Follow #teachlivingpoets, @ MayaCPopa, and @ nktgill on Twitter and @ poetryisnotaluxury on Instagram.

Poetry books can also provide a way to celebrate the linguistic diversity in your classroom. Every year, I teach several students who speak Russian at home and my bilingual anthology of *Contemporary Russian Poetry* is hard to keep on my shelf. The same is true of my Pablo Neruda collection and *Cool Salsa: Bilingual Poems About Growing Up Latino in the United States* with poems in the original Spanish and the English translation on the facing page.

Through the years, I have invited bilingual students to read poems in their original language and then in their English translation as part of our Poem of the Day routine, and sometimes the translations were even created by my students. I have listened to poetry in Farci and Hungarian, Uzbek and French, Arabic and Ukrainian and Spanish because of these invitations.

Rather than try and replicate the poetry shelf in someone else's classroom library, start your own. Pick five poetry books, purchase them, present them in book talks, and loan them out. Add to these shelves over time. Record student book talks about the poetry and books-in-verse they love so that future students can hear from their peers.

THE DAILY ROUTINE

If you decide to make poetry a daily habit in your own classroom, know that just like any yearlong commitment you want to make, the first year will be the hardest. But it can be done. And over time, it becomes downright simple. Soon, your problem is not where to find poems that take your students where you want them to go, but rather how to pare down your list of 500 into a set of 180 that you can share with them in the space of a school year.

If a year seems daunting, consider starting a Poem of the Day habit during April, National Poetry Month in the United States. For six years I edited a blogging project, *Go Poems*. It contains mini-lesson ideas that do some of the heavy lifting of starting this month-long routine for you, and the lessons come from teachers all over the country. Likely some of them teach in circumstances much like yours. 180 ideas are there waiting for you!

But remember, the best routines will start with you. The American Academy of Poets, Poetry Foundation, *The Writer's Almanac*, *The Slowdown*: all of these sources have a daily poetry e-mail and/or podcast feature that will get you reading poetry with more frequency and expose you to types of poems you might not otherwise spend your time reading. And the great thing about poetry e-mails is that you can read them as you are able and delete them unread when you cannot. Becoming a reader of poetry will be good for your own heart, and soon you will find it brimming with verses to share.

If you make poetry part of your daily routine, you will see that this book is nothing more than one teacher's concept of what works for his students. Naturally, I hope that you will use some activities in this book to get things started in your class. My greater aspiration though is that you find the poems that touch your heart and use some of my limited experience to merge with your own. Find ways to bring those favorite, beautiful words to your students. I hope you get your students thinking, talking, writing, and laughing about poems. I hope there are some uncomfortable silences in your work with poems that allow space for growth. I hope you help your students transfer the skills they grow in a practice of poetry pauses to the dreams and demands of their other writing goals and priorities.

I hope your own habit of poetry reading inspires you to write some of your own poems.

HELPING STUDENTS KEEP UP THE HABIT

Two years after Josh sat in my class, I had the chance to catch up with him after school when he and a friend walked across the parking lot that runs between the high school building and the middle school building where I teach.

After a bit of small talk, Josh said to me, "So, Mr. Vogelsinger, do you remember telling us that one day we were going to wake up with an empty feeling inside?"

Taken aback, I paused a beat, then stammered, "Really? That doesn't sound like me." I scolded myself: *Brett, why would you ever say this to a student?*

"Oh, it was definitely you," he reminded me. "At the end of the year, when we were finishing up Poem of the Day, you told us one day over the summer we'd wake up with that empty feeling, missing that routine of a poem every day."

I smiled, relaxing. "Oh, OK. Maybe I did say it in that context!"

"Well, you were right," Josh told me. "It happened. And I went to those websites you shared on your teacher website and signed up for the e-mails. I really missed having a poem in my life every day."

These moments happen to all teachers, when we learn we have had an impact that lives beyond our classroom. Josh was not the last student to specifically mention Poem of the Day when visiting me, to tell me how much they loved or missed it, to express that they wished other teachers kept the same habit. It has become a signature move in my teaching, and one that has a lasting impact on students.

Help your student to find a favorite poet who speaks to them during the year. Is it a slam champion on YouTube or an Instapoet? Is it a poet from thousands of miles or hundreds of years away? Is it a contemporary poet calling for social justice, or a nature poet savoring the peace we acquire by patient observation of the world around us?

When we help our students acquire their own taste in poems, we set them up to find more poems without us. When we show them how poetry pauses can help them develop a wide spectrum of writing skills, we make sure that our instruction and the mentorship of the poems we choose have a lasting impact in their lives.

Can we help our students to see and hear the poetry in everything they write? Can we help them follow Verlyn Klinkenborg's (2013) advice: "Pay attention to rhythm, first and last" (p. 1)? How will this help them craft a lab report, a résumé, a scholarship application, an essay, a letter to the editor?

Can reading and writing poetry as a student lead them to a life full of noticing and a life full of vivid language? Can it help them become more compelling storytellers in whatever career path they choose?

How Does a Poetry Routine Help?
What Students Say

Michael:

One Poem of the Day that helped me was "Coming Home at Twilight in Late Summer" by Jane Kenyon. This poem made me realize that I needed to pay attention to the finer details when my writing was rather bland. I could visualize every part of her poem, but when I went back to my writing, I couldn't. So I sought to change that.

I decided to write a short story . . . about a man coming home to his house after a zombie apocalypse. I focused on the vast empty corridors, paint chipping off the walls, and an old, cracked picture of his family on the floor. This poem helped me become a better writer by making me squeeze the finer details from my writing.

Lila:

Reading so many poems this year has helped me realize how much I truly enjoy writing poetry. I've written a few poems and stories already, and I still have ideas for each of them floating around in my head. Writing so many poems has also helped me write new poetry with more ease than I had before. Additionally, the first writing assessment helped me learn good revising and editing skills as well as the importance of figurative language.

In the majority of my poems, I enjoy using figurative language because I feel it adds depth to the poem, making it more interesting. Knowing how to correctly revise and edit a writing piece is also important because it can make your writing so much better. In order for me to finish writing all of my poems and stories I have started, I need to start picking one to two stories/poems to expand on each week instead of starting completely new stories every few days. This way, my poems and stories will be complete, allowing me to come up with new ideas.

Hana:

I've really enjoyed reading each poem of the day, and I think they have helped me expand as a reader and writer a lot. It has expanded my vocabulary because a lot of the poems have used very unique words. Also, these poems have made me think a lot since poems are usually written so the reader has to think and create their own meaning of it. Having to think and analyze what I've read also helps me to problem-solve better and be able to understand more complex writing.

One of my favorite poems that we've read had to be "Invitation" by Shel Silverstein. I really enjoyed this poem because of the inclusiveness it gave out and how it made me think but not too hard about the meaning. This poem also inspired me to write in more creative ways using things such as repetition, punctuation, and much more. I also enjoyed these poems because they spark a lot of ideas and give me things to write about in my writer's notebook.

Nousha (a former student and recent college graduate):

I wish creative writing was imposed as much as professional/essay writing. Though I have used more professional writing in college and while working, it doesn't mean creative writing doesn't have its uses.
I think school in general does little to foster creativity. English is one of the few classes where you can express some sense of yourself. . . .
Writing creatively means you can tell a story, and the better you are at it, the more eyes you can capture. I have talked to many hiring managers while networking, and all have told me they want a candidate that can tell a story about their aspirations and their journey. However, these candidates are lacking, because although we learn how to read stories, we aren't taught how to tell them.

POETRY PAUSE: THE FEEDBACK HAIKU

When it comes to student writing, we have all had the experience of returning work, replete with comments we spent our weekend writing or recording or whatever manner we choose for our feedback, only to watch students give it a cursory glance and move on. How can poetry help with this?

Enter the feedback haiku.

I first asked students to write a feedback haiku on a whim. We were finishing up a marking period, and I felt like we needed something to synopsize our learning. There were so many good bits of growth in the marking period, but it felt fractured and scattered.

So I took half a class period and said, "Remember in elementary school when you would write haiku poems? They are the Japanese form that uses five syllables in the first line, seven in the second line and five in the third. Here's one written by the master haiku poet, Basho." And this is where I snuck in the Poem of the Day.

"I challenge you: Go back into our LMS and look over all your feedback on the assignments from this marking period. I'll project a list of the assignments I'm talking about on the screen. As you do so, try to winnow down everything I've shared with you to help promote growth, to give you praise and critique, and get it down to just three lines, 5-7-5, a 'feedback haiku.' Extra kudos if you can use ONLY words I used in giving feedback. Shape it into something that encapsulates what I gave back to you and preserve it on a page in your writer's notebook where you'll get a chance to see it many times before the year ends."

The results were wonderful. Students were excited to share their creations, sometimes even burning me with a critique that sounded pretty harsh when reduced to just a few syllables. The poems provided a mirror for me. What am I saying to students about their work? Am I giving them what they need to get better?

Three Sample Feedback Haiku From My Students

These haikus are based on feedback on a personal narrative piece.

stick with the past tense
great participial phrase here
enough shifts to split

Jack D.

Drawing out time here
Love the rhythm in this piece
Reflection and voice

Alexis T.

Would love a gesture
You capture eyes of child
Fun hyperbole

Michelle M.

WRITING OURSELVES OUT OF A CORNER

Poetry gives us many things, but most of all it gives us freedom. There are endless forms a poem can take. One form is so open to possibility, it is in the name: free verse. Poems do not have to rhyme. No topics are off-limits. Sometimes they capture beauty, and sometimes they confront us with ugliness. Former U.S. Poet Laureate Tracy K. Smith (2021) calls poems "offerings of desperately needed hope and endurance" (p. xxiii).

Whatever we need to say, a poem can be our megaphone. And whatever we need to say to ourselves, a poem can be a pair of AirPods, turned down low, whispering to us in our ear as the rest of the world passes by, unknowing.

The poems we write help us to know ourselves. A beautiful, tiny poem by Hayden Saunier reminds us of this:

I NEED TO LIVE NEAR A CREEK

by Hayden Saunier

because
the lush

mossy
rush of it

hushes
me up.

From *How to Wear This Body* by Hayden Saunier. Terrapin Books, 2017.

Poems help us to pinpoint what hushes us, what brings us solace, what helps us find peace in a world of troubles. When I read this poem with students, we all write a poem in response that begins with two simple words: "I need." Where can those two words take us?

I recently came across a beautiful paragraph about the power of poems by writer Angela Hugunin (2020). She reflects, "I've lost count of how many times poems have settled my internal storms. They've let me sit with my sadness, ponder it, and almost befriend it. They've humbled me by giving me a window into the pain of others. They've restrained me from assuming I can grasp things with utmost certainty; they've reminded me that this world is far from static" (para. 7).

And sometimes, as writers and as human beings, life does begin to feel uncomfortably static. We find ourselves in a corner. We get stuck. We do not know what to do or how to say something necessary. Sometimes what keeps us cornered is beyond our control, and sometimes the corner is a dark place to inhabit.

Our students find themselves in these corners too. As Derek Thompson (2022) reports in *The Atlantic*, "From 2009 to 2021, the share of American high-school students who say they feel 'persistent feelings of sadness or hopelessness' rose from 26 percent to 44 percent, according to a new CDC study. This is the highest level of teenage sadness ever recorded" (para. 1). Teachers know this. We see the effects of it daily. And we often feel underqualified to help students to cope.

Poems of Light and Hope

1. "Everything Is Going to Be All Right" by Derek Mahon
2. "Small Kindnesses" by Danusha Laméris
3. "won't you celebrate with me" by Lucille Clifton
4. "Boarding House" by Ted Kooser
5. "Kindness" by Steven Dunn
6. "Complainers" by Rudy Francisco
7. "Shake the Dust" by Anis Mojgani
8. "Something About the Wind" by Sidney Hall Jr.
9. "The Human Family" by Maya Angelou
10. "Whale Day" by Billy Collins
11. "For the Bird Singing Before Dawn" by Kim Stafford
12. "Instructions on Not Giving Up" by Ada Limón

IT ALL COMES DOWN TO THIS

Poems allow us to move within and eventually out of these corners. They let us start anywhere on the blank page, not just the top left-hand corner. They let us manipulate the white space to get us where we need to go. They let us type a few quick lines in the notes section of our phones. They let in the sliver of light we need to keep going.

Writing them gives us an escape hatch. Reading them gives us companionship.

In this book, we have talked about tilting the page, breaking text into new forms, rambling in lists, and blacking things out. We have talked about musing over a needful fact and shrinking feedback into haiku.

Pausing with poems enriches our classrooms, certainly. I have seen it. But it also enriches our lives.

Dear reader, be well, take care of yourself, bring poetry to your students, and be in touch. I wish you the best on your journey with many pauses for poetry along the way.

APPENDIX A
STRATEGIES TO
STREAMLINE AND
SCAFFOLD

Great teachers like you know that sometimes a class, a student, or a group of students may need a more streamlined version of a lesson for it to go smoothly. Others may need a scaffold to help them achieve without debilitating frustration.

These best practices are great ideas for any classroom, and throughout the book, sidebars suggest which strategies might work for specific lessons or poems in the book. I hope you find them helpful!

STREAMLINING STRATEGIES

1. **Use an excerpt of the poem instead of the entire poem.** This can magnify the element of the poem you want to work with in class and pull away lines or parts of the poem that could be overwhelming. When making this choice, always include "excerpt from" before the title on your slide or handout. Use this method judiciously. The same way we never want short-passage reading to usurp whole-book reading in an English class curriculum, we want to avoid the habit of using only part of a poem lest students miss practice in pulling out the important bits of full-length pieces.

2. If discussion of poetry is new, slow, or stilted, **try a think aloud**, modeling the way readers can approach a poem as a reader. When doing this, it is important not to sound like an expert, but rather to let them hear your first-time-reader thoughts. "When I get to

this line/image/word, I really start to wonder . . ." and "It seems like the poem takes an intriguing turn here when . . ." are two good lines to include in a think aloud because they model that you appreciate uncertainty and embrace ambiguity in the opening discussion of a poem. Show students what it is like to construct an idea as you speak. In other classes, students may be conditioned to raise their hand only when they are certain they have the right answer. Demonstrate that divergent, emergent, and evolving thoughts are welcome. After thinking aloud and modeling this a few times in class, watch how your students are more willing to take the risk to jump in and participate in discussions.

3. **Use a video or audio clip of the poem read by a professional reader or by the poet.** This can be useful for a few reasons. First, the intonations and voice quality will be audible, fluent, and heartfelt. The reader will pause and modulate well and provide an excellent model for both you and your students. Sometimes when we listen to poets read their own work, something stands out that we might have missed on the page. Second, it allows for self-paced work when students are in the thick of a project, book club, or online learning. When we cannot or do not want to have the whole class united in traditional ways, audio and video of poetry reading are available online to help us out. Third, some recordings such as *The Slowdown Podcast* or the *Ours Poetica* collection on YouTube will provide just a pinch of context or reader response to the poem that models good thinking and provides an entry point to the poem.

4. **Explicitly share *what* you will be doing with the poem and *why* you will be doing it** at the start of the lesson or mini-lesson. A quick 1,2,3 outline works for me. "First we will read this poem, keeping an eye on this particular aspect. Second, we will take this action together, and third we will take this action as individuals. Our goal is to . . ." This simple frame, often paired with a quick list on the whiteboard, projects good organization, shares the "why" with students right from the start, and provides an anchor so students can see their progress. This is considered best practice in many classrooms, and some teachers are required to have an agenda or outlined objectives on the board to review with students at the start of class. There are certainly days when I do not share every detail of where we are headed with a poem so that we can ride the wave of it together, discovering things along the way. But if you feel like focus is lacking in the class, being more explicit will help streamline by keeping you and your students on track and out of the weeds.

SCAFFOLDING STRATEGIES

1. **Start a draft of a poem together as a class**, modeling how to follow a pattern, form, or mentor text. Then, after students have copied the lines you began crafting together, let each continue the draft in their own notebooks. Share their work briefly in pairs or table groups so that the students have a chance to see how their peers have continued to build on the initial lines.

2. **Create a fill-in-the blank version of the poem** by typing up a copy, hollowing out the core content, and preserving the structure of the original poem. Project this on the screen or print half-sheets for students to tape in their notebooks. For students who struggle or have little experience working with mentor texts, this can be a great warm-up to the concept, helping them to see the poem as something that is built or crafted around specific structural choices. This strategy ends up creating a copy-change poem, and the technique is modeled a few times throughout the book.

3. **"Think, Pair, Share"** is an old strategy but a good one. When we have students jot something down during the "think" part of this activity, even if it is a sentence or quick list that takes a minute or less to create, we allow them to organize their own thoughts. When we briefly pair up with another student to speak our thinking, it allows students to test-drive an idea before they share it with the class. Suddenly sharing with the whole class becomes less intimidating because it has already happened in miniature. Use this strategy to scaffold class discussion of a poem you read.

4. **Substitute a children's poem.** Keep *Where the Sidewalk Ends* by Shel Silverstein and an anthology of children's poetry nearby. Tag Amy Ludwig VanDerwater's *The Poem Farm* website as a favorite in your browser. Subscribe to Irene Latham's e-mail newsletter. Children's poets provide the ultimate scaffolding for any skill you are teaching with the methods in this book. If the suggested poems mentioned in the book ever feel like they will be too cumbersome for your student, seek out a poem that is written for a younger audience and has the same type of gem to share. I have found these poems, though simpler in language and syntax, are delightfully rich even as an adult reader, and some examples of my favorites to use in the classroom take center stage in the lessons in this book.

5. **Show your sample.** Quickly create an exemplar live, or create one before class begins so the pressure is off. Never underestimate

the power of students knowing that their teacher writes. This is a best practice for any writing teacher. However, I include this here as a scaffold because showing how you completed the assignment affirms that it can be done, demonstrates that you enjoyed it, and provides a second mentor text for students. There are times that the teacher exemplar is especially important because you can tailor your model to the needs of the students and the assignment in front of you.

6. **Start with a visual aid for some context.** Sometimes a picture to illustrate an unfamiliar word, a photograph to bring readers into a setting, or a map to orient the poem geographically can help readers understand the poem more thoroughly before we use it to improve our writing.

APPENDIX B
REPRODUCIBLE
HANDOUTS

ANALYSIS

Name: _____

Directions: Use this template to write a poem about your topic, gathering up all of the many things your book, movie, or album is about.

_____ is not just about _____.

It's about _____,

_____,

_____.

It's about _____ and

_____.

It's about _____

and _____ and _____.

CHARACTER AND CONFLICT

Name: _____

Directions: Using Janet Wong's poem "Sisters" as a template, create your own poem to write about the relationship between two characters in the book you are reading.

He/she/they says/say that I am _____

because I am so _____,

_____.

I wish I were _____

and _____, like _____,

like _____.

NOVEL ANALYSIS

Name: _____

Directions: The diagram on this page was created by psychologist Robert Plutchik to map out human emotions and how they relate to each other. As you read your novel, follow two characters. Briefly record the emotional state for each of these characters on the wheel at least four times as you read the book. Each time, write a one-sentence note explaining what puts the character in this emotional state. Later in the unit, we will use this information to draw some conclusions about this book.

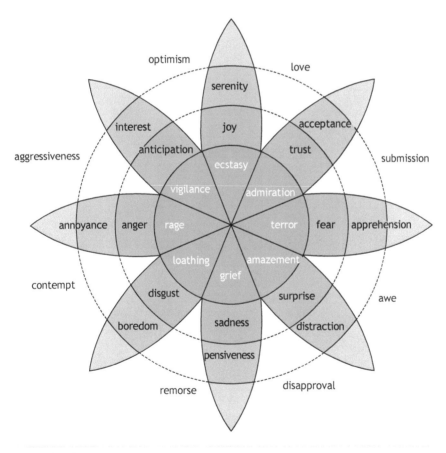

Public domain.

IMAGERY FOR NARRATIVE WRITING

Name: _____

Directions: The two windowpane organizers on this page will help use visualization, first as a reading skill, then as a writing skill.

Sketch four images from the poem we read together in class in the windowpane organizer below.

Poem Title _____ Poet _____

Now, turn the page over to work on some visualization to help you as a writer!

Sketch four key images from the story that you are telling in your narrative piece. What are the four images you want readers to remember most from your writing?

As you return to your draft, craft scenes, paragraphs, and sentences that will make these images stand out, making the reader feel like they are in the scene with you.

STANZAS AND PARAGRAPHING

Name: _____

Directions: To help us think about shifts in focus within a single piece of writing, let's study how Sara Teasdale breaks her ideas into stanzas in the poem "Winter Stars." This poem was written in response to World War I.

It is interesting to know that the word *stanza* comes from the Italian word for "room." So each stanza in the poem is like a smaller room within the larger structure.

After we read it out loud twice, let's jot down some ideas in the margins about each stanza's main idea. We'll watch how she uses stanzas to show us slight shifts in focus. Then we will discuss how paragraphs work much the same way in other types of writing.

WINTER STARS

by Sara Teasdale

I went out at night alone;
 The young blood flowing beyond the sea
Seemed to have drenched my spirit's wings—
 I bore my sorrow heavily.

But when I lifted up my head
 From shadows shaken on the snow,
I saw Orion in the east
 Burn steadily as long ago.

From windows in my father's house,
 Dreaming my dreams on winter nights,
I watched Orion as a girl
 Above another city's lights.

Years go, dreams go, and youth goes too,
 The world's heart breaks beneath its wars,
All things are changed, save in the east
 The faithful beauty of the stars.

Source: *Flame and Shadow* (1920). Public domain.

PARALLEL STRUCTURE

Name: _____

Directions: After we read part of Alex Dimitrov's poem, "Love" out loud, try crafting your own parallel lines that each begin with the same two simple words: "I love."

See where this takes you!

I love _____

I love _____

I love _____

I love _____

I love _____

I love _____

I love _____

I love _____

I love _____

I love _____

I love _____

I love _____

PREPOSITION POEMS

Name: _____

Directions: From the left side of chart below, choose a title that might be fun to work with. Then write a poem in which each line begins with a different preposition from the right side of the chart.

Preposition Poem Writing

• Where Is My Other Sock?	• about • above • across • against • along • amid	• in • inside • into • near • on
• Where Is Love?	• among • around	• onto • over
• Where Has Childhood Gone?	• at • behind	• past • through
• Where Do Dreams Come From?	• below • beneath • beside	• toward • under • up
• Places to Look for the Meaning of Life	• between • beyond • by	• upon • with • within

APPENDIX C
QUOTABLES

Sometimes to spark a lesson, some notebook writing, or a review of a concept, all it takes is a powerful quote. Here are some quotes gathered from throughout this book that might be useful, even frameable, in your classroom.

I follow the sounds. —Christian Wiman

Fill your paper with the breathings of your heart. —William Wordsworth

Poetry is language at its most distilled and powerful. —Rita Dove

Even if you don't think you have things to say, you do. There are stories only you can tell. —Katherine Schulten

Without poetry, especially when I was younger, being a writer would have seemed like a futile attempt. The poets taught me the functionality of language. —Jason Reynolds

Our world, so worn and weary,
 Needs music, pure and strong,
To hush the jangle and discords
 Of sorrow, pain, and wrong.
—Frances Ellen Watkins Harper

Raise your words
not your voice.
It's rain that grows flowers,
not thunder.
—Rumi

No man is an island. —John Donne

The elegance of argument lives in poetry. —Glenda Funk

Poetry and science have grown up together
as siblings . . . they are closer together than they
are apart. —Alicia Sometimes

You can find moving, rich language in books, on walls,
even in junk mail. —Stephen Dunning and William Stafford

In reality, every piece of writing is a custom job,
not a modular home. —John Warner

Be sure you know the structure of all you
wish to depict. —Leonardo da Vinci

Imagine it this way: One by one, each sentence takes the stage. It says the very thing it comes into existence to say. Then it leaves the stage. —Verlyn Klinkenborg

Poetry is all nouns and verbs. —Marianne Moore

I'm not a very good writer, but I'm an excellent rewriter. —James Michener

Poetry is an act of attention. —D. H. Lawrence

Poetry is a bit like lacing a pair of shoes. You have to wind things together, pull them tight, tie a knot or two and combine things that might feel impossible the first few times but could eventually come together in a stronger whole . . . —Gregory Welch

Poems are "offerings of desperately needed hope and endurance." —Tracy K. Smith

I've lost count of how many times poems have settled my internal storms. —Angela Hugunin

STUDENT WORK CITED

Afsgar, Nousha. Survey response.

Bastien, Leo. Preposition poem.

Birkhead, Luke. Poem.

Borelli, Sienna. Poem.

Brackbill, Owen. Student classwork.

Brestovitskiy, Jessica. Poem.

Carter, Ryan. Student classwork.

Cherry, Gavin. Golden Shovel poem.

deHoogh, John. Feedback haiku.

Friend, William. Poem.

Frye, Michael. Student classwork.

Ganopolskiy, Andrew. Golden Shovel poem.

Gordon, Madison. "I Hate Personal Narratives."

Gordon, Maximus. Found poem.

Julien, Remy. Preposition poem.

Junkin, Mackenzie. Artwork inspired by "Ozymandias."

LaDow, Hana. Survey response.

Leff, Ava. Student classwork.

Lynch, Colin. Word Collection poem.

Imperato, Susana. Response to a poem.

Mackewicz, Hannah. Poem.

Maddox, Brook. Poem.

Maio, Anthony. "The Summer Tree."

Matich, Mason. Response to a poem.

Mehta, Aum. Artwork.

Melnikov, Michelle. Feedback haiku.

Nielson, Lauren. "Autobiography of a Reader."

Pearson, Christian. Student classwork.

Ripp, Ava. Student classwork.

Scully, Rosaleen. Abecedarian poem.

Sharkey, Liam. "Sweat Stain."

Staude, Lila. Survey response.

Steitz, Michael. Survey response.

To, Alexis. Feedback haiku.

Vosgerichian, Amy. Poems.

Wan, Charley. Blackout poem.

Watters, Mackenzie. Abecedarian poem.

Wu, Jason. Essay excerpt.

Young, Jaden. "Exercises for a Hockey Player."

REFERENCES

Introduction: Purposeful Poetry Pauses

Anderson, A. (2020). Helping students see themselves as writers: Creative writing exercises in the writing center. *WLN: A Journal of Writing Center Scholarship, 44*(9-10). https://link .gale.com/apps/doc/A625408568/PROF?u=pl1961r&sid=PROF&xid=902ac301

Atwell, N., Kajder, S., and Rief, L. (2013, November 23). *From the middle: Working with writer's workshop* [Conference presentation]. National Council of Teachers of English Convention, Boston, MA.

Baroudy, I. (2008). Process writing: Successful and unsuccessful writers; discovering writing behaviours. *International Journal of English Studies, 8*(2). https://link.gale.com/apps/doc/ A208536045/PROF?u=pl1961r&sid=PROF&xid=61f89b6c

Bernabei, G., & Van Prooyen, L. (2020). *Text structures from poetry: Lessons to help students read, analyze, and create poems they will remember.* Corwin.

Garber, M. (2018, August 20). Poetry is everywhere. *The Atlantic.* https://www.theatlantic .com/entertainment/archive/2018/08/when-poetry-isnt-poetry/567571/

Illingworth, S. (2022, April 11). How poetry can help communicate science to a more diverse audience. *The Conversation.* https://theconversation.com/ how-poetry-can-help-communicate-science-to-a-more-diverse-audience-180749

Jago, C. (2019). *The book in question.* Heinemann.

Lazarus, E. (2017, October 1). Writing takes work. *Nature.* https://www.nature.com/articles/ nj7675-291a.pdf?origin=ppub

Lund, E. (2021, April 13). How is a sonnet like the suburbs? Both are places of possibility. *Christian Science Monitor.* https://www.csmonitor.com/Books/Author-Q-As/2021/0413/ How-is-a-sonnet-like-the-suburbs-Both-are-places-of-possibility

Osowiecka, M., & Kolanczyk, A. (2018). Let's read a poem! What type of poetry boosts creativity? *Frontiers in Psychology, 9,* 1781. https://www.frontiersin.org/articles/10.3389/ fpsyg.2018.01781/full

Sheldrake, M. (2020). *Entangled life: How fungi make our world, change our minds, and shape our future.* Random House.

Wassiliwizky, E., Koelsch, S., Wagner, V., Jacobsen, T., & Menninghaus, W. (2017). The emotional power of poetry: Neural circuitry, psychophysiology and compositional principles. *Social Cognitive and Affective Neuroscience, 12*(8), 1229-1240. https://www.ncbi.nlm.nih .gov/pmc/articles/PMC5597896/

Wong, J., & Vardell, S. (2017). *Here we go: A poetry Friday power book.* Pomelo Books.

Chapter 1: Poetry to Bring on the Brainstorm

Hicks, T., & Schoenborn, A. (2020). *Creating confident writers.* Norton.

Hughes, T. (1970). *Poetry is*. Doubleday.

Kittle, P. (2008). *Write beside them: Risk, voice, and clarity in high school writing*. Heinemann.

O'Dell, R., & Marchetti, A. (2018). *Beyond literary analysis*. Heinemann.

Pinsky, R. (2014). *Singing school: Learning to write (and read) poetry by studying with the masters*. Norton.

Rief, L. (2018). *The quickwrite handbook*. Heinemann.

Teicher, C. M. (2018). *We begin in gladness: How poets progress*. Graywolf Press.

Chapter 2: Poetry Pauses for Writing Analysis

Adams, M., King, A. S., McCollom-Clark, K., & White, E. (2019, November 22). *Emotion at the center: Narrative, vulnerability, and community in the English classroom* [Conference presentation]. NCTE Convention, , Baltimore, MD.

Bachman, G. (2000, January). Brainstorming deluxe. *Training & Development, 54*(1). https://go.gale.com/ps/i.do?p=AONE&u=googlescholar&id=GALE|A59138066&v=2.1&it=r&sid=AONE&asid=47b5c15e

Ribay, R. (2019). *Patron saints of nothing*. Kokila.

Chapter 3: Poetry Pauses for Crafting Narrative

Blomain, K. (2005). *Greatest hits 1985-2005*. Pudding House.

Cheaney, J. (2020, February 29). Grace and poetry. *World*. https://wng.org/articles/grace-and-poetry-1617297824

Collins, B. (2016, July 20). *Billy Collins reads Eamon Grennan* [Audio podcast interview; P. Muldoon, Host]. *The New Yorker: Poetry*. https://www.newyorker.com/podcast/poetry/billy-collins-reads-eamon-grennan

Green, J. (2019, September 19). John Green reads "Poetry" [Video]. Poetry Foundation, *Ours Poetica* series. YouTube. https://www.poetryfoundation.org/video/151040/john-green-reads-poetry

Harjo, J. (2020, August 14). *Remember: Poetry read along with Poet Laureate Joy Harjo* [Video]. PBS KIDS. YouTube. https://www.youtube.com/watch?v=FYDi_op-92c

Owens, D. (2019, January 8). Delia Owens, author of *Where the Crawdads Sing* [Audio podcast interview; Z. Owens, Host]. *Moms Don't Have Time to Read Books*. https://www.momsdonthavetimetoreadbooks.com/transcripts/specialepisodedeliaowens

Reynolds, J. (2017). Afterword/interview. In *Long way down* [Audiobook]. Simon & Schuster.

Reynolds, J. (2018, June 18). The antidote to hopelessness. *Articulate*. PBS. https://www.pbs.org/video/antidote-hopelessness-1l5uh3/

Schulten, K. (2020, September 9). Coming of age in 2020: A special multimedia contest for teenagers in the U.S. *The New York Times* Learning Network. https://www.nytimes.com/2020/09/09/learning/coming-of-age-in-2020-a-special-multimedia-contest-for-teenagers-in-the-us.html

Storr, W. (2020). *The science of storytelling*. Abrams.

Williams, M. E. (2019, March 18). Laurie Halse Anderson on writing "outside of your lane": "Be prepared to do years of extra work." *Salon*. https://www.salon.com/2019/03/18/laurie-halse-anderson-on-writing-outside-of-your-lane-do-years-of-extra-work/

Chapter 4: Poetry Pauses for Argument Writing

Common Core State Standards Initiative. (n.d.). *English language arts standards: Writing grade 9-10.* https://learning.ccsso.org/wp-content/uploads/2022/11/ELA_Standards1.pdf

Forché, C., Espada, M., & Francis, V. (2020, October 23). *Imagine a new way* [Panel discussion]. The Geraldine Dodge Poetry Festival.

Funk, G. (2020, September 1). Poetry pushes back #SOL20. *Evolving English Teacher.* http://evolvingenglishteacher.blogspot.com/search?q=poetry+argument

Gansworth, E. (2020). *Apple, skin to core.* Levine Querido.

John, A. (2020, June 17). Collar that cat! *The New York Times* Learning Network. https://www.nytimes.com/2020/06/17/learning/collar-the-cat.html

Marshell, K. (2016, April 27). *Voicing counterpoint.* Poetry Foundation. https://www.poetryfoundation.org/articles/89226/voicing-counterpoint

Perdomo, W. (2020). *The breakbeat poets: LatiNext* (Vol. 4). Haymarket Books.

Reach, K. (2013). *Ten nights on Long Island: The Great Gatsby's early reviews.* Melville House. https://www.mhpbooks.com/ten-nights-on-long-island-the-great-gatsbys-early-reviews/

Schulten, K. (Ed.). (2020). *Student voice: 100 argument essays by teens on issues that matter to them.* Norton.

Segal, C. (Producer). (2015, July 10). A detail you may not have known about Eric Garner blossoms in a poem. *PBS News Hour.* https://www.pbs.org/newshour/arts/poetry/small-needful-fact-eric-garner

Chapter 5: Poetry Pauses for Writing Informative and Research Pieces

Alter, A. (2021, January 21). Amanda Gorman captures the moment in verse. *The New York Times.* https://www.nytimes.com/2021/01/19/books/amanda-gorman-inauguration-hill-we-climb.html

Badke, W. (2015). Teaching research skills: Precise, linear path or messy jungle running? *Online Searcher, 39*(6), 71-73.

Burke, J. (2020). *The six academic writing assignments.* Heinemann.

Dunning, S., & Stafford, W. (1992). *Getting the knack: 20 poetry writing exercises.* National Council of Teachers of English.

Gelb, M. J. (1998). *How to think like Leonardo da Vinci: Seven steps to genius every day.* Random House.

Larimer, K., & Gannon, M. (2020). *The poet and writer's complete guide to being a writer.* Avid Reader Press.

Mehta, J., & Fine, S. (2019, March 30). High school doesn't have to be boring. *The New York Times.* https://www.nytimes.com/2019/03/30/opinion/sunday/fix-high-school-education.html

Merriam-Webster. (n.d.). *Merriam-Webster.com* dictionary. https://www.merriam-webster.com/dictionary

Pink, D. (2005). *A whole new mind.* Penguin.

Roessing, L. (2019, February). *After-reading response: Using found poetry for synthesizing text.* Association for Middle Level Education. https://www.amle.org/after-reading-response-using-found-poetry-for-synthesizing-text/

Sometimes, A. (2020, March 13). *Honouring your wonder: Observing the world through art and science* [Video]. Tedx Talks. YouTube. https://www.youtube.com/watch?v=Q6u_F2twb2Y

Warner, J. (2018). *Why they can't write: Killing the five-paragraph essay and other necessities.* Johns Hopkins University Press.

Warner, J. (2019). *The writer's practice: Building confidence in your nonfiction writing.* Penguin Random House.

Welch, G. (2020, July 20). Research won't steal from your poetry. *The Brave Writer.* Medium. https://medium.com/the-brave-writer/research-wont-steal-from-your-poetry-b35089340ea6

Chapter 6: Poetry for Improving Grammar and Punctuation Skills

Bergmann, L. S., & Zepernick, J. (2007). Disciplinarity and transfer: Students' perceptions of learning to write. *Writing Program Administration, 31* (1-2),124-149. http://link.gale.com/apps/doc/A242454181/PROF?u=pl1961r&sid=PROF&xid=d6dcbe7d

Gabbert, E. (2020, December 29). How poets use punctuation as a superpower and a secret weapon. *The New York Times.* https://www.nytimes.com/2020/12/29/books/review/on-poetry-punctuation.html

Hazelton, R. (2013, August 27). *Adventures in anaphora.* Poetry Foundation. https://www.poetryfoundation.org/articles/70030/adventures-in-anaphora

Klinkenborg, V. (2012). *Several short sentences about writing.* Knopf.

Renard, J. (2010). *Nature stories* (D. Parmée, Trans.). New York Review Books Classics.

Sacher, C. L. O. (2016). The writing crisis and how to address it through developmental writing classes. *Research and Teaching in Developmental Education, 32*(2), 46-61. http://link.gale.com/apps/doc/A455286117/PROF?u=pl1961r&sid=PROF&xid=c6c77643

Chapter 7: Poetry as A Healthy Literacy Routine

Hugunin, A. (2020, April 7). *The comforts of a poem: Reflections on Mary Oliver's "Mysteries, Yes."* The Chipewa Valley Writer's Guild, Eau Claire, WI. http://www.cvwritersguild.org/writing-the-valley-1/2020/4/7/the-comfort-of-a-poem-reflections-on-mary-olivers-mysteries-yes

Klinkenborg, V. (2013). *Several short sentences about writing.* Penguin Random House.

Smith, T. K. (Ed.). (2021). *The best American poetry, 2021.* Scribner.

Thompson, D. (2022, April 11). Why American teens are so sad. *The Atlantic.* https://www.theatlantic.com/newsletters/archive/2022/04/american-teens-sadness-depression-anxiety/629524/

Welch, G. (2020, March 30). Write your poetry one line at a time. *Medium.* https://medium.com/swlh/write-your-poetry-one-line-at-a-time-952971eab4f6

INDEX

A SAGE Publishing Company

CORWIN HAS ONE MISSION: to enhance education through intentional professional learning.

We build long-term relationships with our authors, educators, clients, and associations who partner with us to develop and continuously improve the best evidence-based practices that establish and support lifelong learning.

Because...

ALL TEACHERS ARE LEADERS

AFRIKA AFENI MILLS

This guide explores why racial identity work is crucial, especially for White-identifying students and teachers, and guides educators to provide opportunities for antiracist learning.

ALLISON SKERRETT, PETER SMAGORINSKY

Engage students in critical thinking, literacy activities, and inquiry using the personal and social issues of pressing importance to today's students.

MARIA WALTHER

This resource offers a scaffolding for moving from teacher-led demonstration of read alouds to student-led discovery of literacy skills—across the bridge of shared reading.

VERA AHIYYA

Spark courageous conversations with children about race, identity, and social justice using read alouds as an entry point.

To order your copies, visit corwin.com/literacy

At Corwin Literacy we have put together a collection of just-in-time, classroom-tested, practical resources from trusted experts that allow you to quickly find the information you need when you need it.

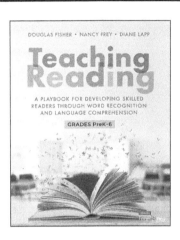

DOUGLAS FISHER, NANCY FREY, DIANE LAPP

Like an animated encyclopedia, this book delivers the latest evidence-based practices in 13 interactive modules that will transform your instruction and reenergize your career.

JUSTIN M. STYGLES

Learn how to build relationships so shame-bound readers trust enough to risk enough to grow.

GRETCHEN BERNABEI, JAYNE HOVER

Use these lessons and concrete text structures designed to help students write self-generated commentary in response to reading.

CHRISTINA NOSEK, MELANIE MEEHAN, MATTHEW JOHNSON, MATTHEW R. KAY, DAVE STUART JR.

This series offers actionable answers to your most pressing questions about teaching reading, writing, and ELA.